D0547552

Nobody's Poodle

Nikki and Richard Attree

Illustrations by Annie Chapman

Nobody's Poodle

Copyright © 2013 Nikki and Richard Attree
All rights reserved.

www.nobodyspoodle.com

ISBN-13:978-1481912990
ISBN-10:1481912992

Contents

For the late, great Basil (Sr. el Baz) - a Very Special Dog, and the original
SpokesMutt for www.TenerifeDogs.com

"I am Nobody's Poodle
But I'm Somebody's Doodle,
And I Woof … therefore I Am!"

CHAPTER ONE
The Dog Bowl of Life

As usual it was raining when I opened my eyes. Another typical summer day in England - cold and wet. Woof-Bloody-Tastic, maybe there'll be some mud to roll around in. Yet again those pesky pussies had been up-and-at-it all night with their infernal racket - no shame those pussies. So I was feeling a bit 'ruff', same as it ever was ... but something was different this morning.

There's been a lot of unusual activity in the Gizmo household lately. The humans have been doing strange things - like putting stuff in boxes, and now it seemed to be reaching a peak of frenzy. I went to check that my dog bowl hadn't disappeared into one of the boxes. Nope, it was still there ... phew, that's a relief.

My owners: Sharon, Trev, and the small human: Tracey, have been talking non-stop about "starting a new life" in some place called Tenerife. From what I can gather, 'The Reef' is a small volcanic island stuck out in the Atlantic somewhere off the coast of Africa. The island is apparently very dry and dusty, and has no grass (except on the golf courses). This is a bit of a shame cos I really enjoy a good roll around on wet grass, or even better in some nice fresh cow dung. Unfortunately us dogs can't afford the golf course fees and apparently there aren't any cows roaming around Tenerife. Amazing eh? Anyway, wadever ... I'm a very adaptable pooch and I guess I'll find something else to roll in there. "Go with the Flow" and "Feel the Fur" as us adaptable woofers say.

I had no idea why they wanted to move there, but apparently the weather was better - wall-to-wall sunshine, and they were talking about having lots of "quality time" to enjoy outdoors. Sounds pretty wooftastic to me - lots more walkies, and some sun on my fur when I'm having a nap. Apparently the locals call this a 'siesta', and that worries me a bit. Am I going to be able to communicate with the local woofers? You see, us pooches have a universal language: 'Woof', but I'd have to get used to my new furry amigos' dialect.

Maybe I'd just stick to sniffing butt at first. Woofing very loudly to make yourself understood is considered a bit rude, and only done by stuck-up snobby dogs like Poodles, or thick chav mutts like Pitbulls. Now, I'm nobody's Poodle.

I'm actually what's known as a Doodle* and I'm very much my own dog. I'm also an extremely sophisticated, intelligent pooch (we might as well get that established early in the first chapter), and I want to try and integrate with the locals. You know - learn the lingo, explore the culture, eat lots of garlic ... that kind of thing. So I'm hoping that in time I'll be fluent in Canarian Woof (which is apparently different from the mainland Spanish variety).

So there I was, nicely curled up on the bed, snoring away and enjoying my siesta (may as well get used to the lingo) when this big truck pulled up outside our house. Four men got out and started loading our boxes into the lorry. Now normally, intruders engaged in daylight robbery would be my cue for a big-time woofing opportunity, but as I say, this morning was a bit different. Instead of encouraging me to bark like crazy and scare the shit out of the scoundrels before they stole all our stuff, Sharon was offering them cups of tea and biscuits, and Trev was telling them to "hurry-up mate, cos like we've got a plane to catch".

So I retreated to a corner of the living room, as far away from the chaos as possible, and kept quiet. As I said, I'm a super sensitive pooch and there was enough tension in the air already, without me adding to it with my normal manic woofing. I watched as most of the boxes disappeared into the lorry, and then to my horror I saw Tracey hand them a box labelled

* in fact I'm a 'Lab-Doodle', and if you're intrigued by this, you can find out more about them at www.doodlemania.co.uk.

"Gizmo's Stuff". Oh No! Just as I feared, my dog bowl was being nicked!

I sprinted out of the house, but I was too late. The robbers slammed shut the door of the truck and drove off. My precious bowl had now disappeared into the distance, and they were probably going to sell it. Thieving feckin so-and-so's! Some morning I'm having then ... and the rest of that day didn't get much better.

A few hours later I was dumped in the car and taken off to Chris' house. Apparently he's what's known as a 'dog sitter' (maybe because he keeps telling me to "sit", cos he certainly doesn't do much sitting around himself. Most of the time he's out at work, but anyway wadever ...). I normally get left with him when my humans go on holiday. He's a nice enough bloke, but I always miss my family when they go away. Sharon and Trev waved good-bye and told me they'd see me in a couple of weeks.

A couple of weeks! What's that all about? I'm a feckin dog, and even a super-sophisto pooch like me doesn't have much concept of future time. Or rather, us dogs have a different, slimmed-down, more efficient concept of time. We realize *a long time ago* (ha ha, get it?) that time was more like a small round thing rather than a long thin thing. More like a dog chasing its own tail rather than an endless piece of string, or an infinitely long ladder, or whatever else humans think it's like. For us dogs, the past and future don't actually exist - there is only the present. It's much less confusing to live like that.

Anyway, as they say: wadever ... I didn't really have much say in what was happening, so I gave Tracey (the small human) a farewell lick, and the taller humans my best hard-done-by look.

Time went by in a flash, as it always does for us dogs (like I said, try chasing your own tail - it works!), and the next big day arrived. Chris got me up early. Today I was going to Tenerife ... "Yee-ha Wooftastic!".

A taxi was due to pick me up from Chris' house and take me to the airport. We waited and waited ... finished our breakfast ... and still no sign of the taxi. Chris was getting more and more agitated as he was going to be late for work. Finally he couldn't wait any longer and rang the animal transportation company ('Flying Fur'), who were supposed to have booked the taxi.

Feckin typical! Never mind 'Flying Fur', the fur brains had lost some of my paperwork and didn't even realize I needed to be collected. Now I was going to miss my flight! Chris was a real hero though. He took me to work with him, and arranged for another taxi to pick me up from there. The Flying Fur bimbo said that she'd book me onto a later flight.

In the end I had a really interesting day meeting Chris' work mates. They were all very kind to me and apparently thought that I was a bit of a star (frankly, I'm not surprised). In fact I was having such a good time that I thought about not getting into the taxi, but I knew Tracey would be really sad if I didn't arrive in Tenerife. So I said farewell to my new friends and climbed into the taxi.

The saga wasn't quite over though, and the fur wasn't flying just yet. The taxi driver demanded a hundred-and-forty quid for the journey, but in his haste to leave the house Chris had forgotten the cash. He asked the driver if he could give it to them later, but taxi man said no - he needed paying right now, or this mutt was going nowhere.

I began to panic, but as I say Chris is a hero, and so were his work-mates. They had a quick whip-round and managed to raise the dosh (so I really had worked my charms on this lot - wooftastic!). I was thinking: "scratch my bollox! a hundred-and-forty quid for a fifteen minute journey - this limo must be seriously bling". My tail was wagging like a yo-yo anticipating what I might find: probably a cocktail cabinet of sausages and a cute little bitch to entertain me on the journey. Woof woof - life was finally looking up.

Once inside the taxi though, I was sadly disappointed. No food - not even a solitary dog biscuit, and no sign of a panting poochette waiting for me in the back seat. Just a feckin wooden box with handles and a little door - and guess who that was for ...

So I was shoved in the crate, and eventually arrived at an extremely noisy smelly place (apparently called 'Cat-Wick'). Still in my box, I was wheeled through the airport without even having the chance to sniff around the duty-free section (I was hoping that I might be able to pick up another dog bowl to replace the one the thieving scum-bags in the lorry had taken).

The plane journey was similarly disappointing. I was looking forward to the in-flight meal, but there seemed to be no stewardess service. I'd heard my owners say that the food on planes was "only good enough to give to a bloody dog". In fact I think they actually called it "a dog's dinner". Well that's all-right then. How very considerate of the airline to make meals especially for us dogs. So, where was my dinner then?

Sadly it didn't appear. Not even a feckin complimentary packet of peanuts. Woof-Bloody-Tastic eh? I'd heard that there were now "no frills" on budget airlines, but for goodness sake - they could have given us pooches a few measly peanuts (come to think of it, peanuts aren't too good for us woofers are they?). And here's another thing: my flight actually cost more than a human's ticket! For the price Sharon and Trev paid, I should have been up-graded to 'fur-st class', with my water-bowl being filled the instant it became empty, and tasty snacks arriving each time I raised my paw. But instead, here I was stuck in a bloody cage, not even able to have a shit. I had a water bowl, but that was about it as far as the in-flight entertainment went.

My fellow travellers didn't exactly ease the pain either. Next to me was a Rottweiler called Rambo, and I had to endure his sneering, snarling and spitting for the entire journey. Just behind Rambo there was a rather more luxurious crate containing two Chihuahuas: Fifi and Hilton. They kept yapping on about "the class of dogs you get on these cheap flights", and moaning that they'd never be seen dead "Flying The Fur" ever again.

I couldn't work out whether it was me or the Chihuahuas that was getting up Rambo's nose so much, but just as we started our descent he suddenly started apologising for his bad behaviour. Apparently he suffered from a 'fur of flying' (ironic given the name of the airline), and he wanted us to know that he really loved us all! Moreover, as it was very unlikely that he'd ever see us again, he wanted to share something that he'd never been able to tell another dog.

"Never say never" I thought to myself, "dude, I've got a feeling you're going to regret this".

He told us that his owner insisted on dressing him in macho studded collars and black dog t-shirts with "Watch Out ... I Haven't Eaten Today!" on them; and he only ever took Rambo to the parts of town where even the rats have moved out because it's gone so down-market (hence the expression: "gone to the dogs"). Whereas actually he'd much rather be wearing a pink frilly coat with a matching spangly collar, and strutting his stuff in a chic up-town neighbourhood.

Now I'm not adverse to a spot of accessorising myself. I do sometimes sport a very cool bandanna when I'm out and about town, and Sharon has been known to put a Christmas hat on me - but only once a year, in the privacy of my own home, and then just to take photos. Of course I have no problem with humans giving a pooch some extra protection from the elements, but dressing up dogs in ridiculous looking outfits usually makes me barking mad. In this case though, the cross dressing malarky was Rambo's own predilection. His own little secret, until now anyway.

To be honest, the thought of this hulking great Rottweiler posing in a pink frilly outfit went some way to making me forget the day's many stresses. I was bursting to laugh but I felt sorry for the dude, even if he had made my flight worse than it already was. After all, it couldn't have been easy for a macho mutt like him to come out with a confession like that. The Chihuahuas didn't hold back though. They were rolling around their cage howling with laughter. As we touched down he was trembling and sweating, and they certainly weren't showing him any compassion.

After we'd landed, Rambo was very quiet. I think he was probably regretting telling us his deepest darkest secret, but we didn't have long to say our good-byes before our crates were wheeled into the airport. I could hear the Chihuahuas' manic laughter receding into the distance as they were driven away to a different section of cargo.

Then I heard some familiar voices. "Wow is that my humans? Yes oh yes, that's their smell. Yippee, Woof Woof!". There they were: Sharon, Trev, and Tracey - looking very relieved to see me. I was in doggie heaven, and we had a very emotional reunion in the cargo bay, involving lots of licking of faces and a few tears. Even the tough guys with tattoos working there were touched.

I never saw Rambo's owner, but out of the corner of my eye I glimpsed the Chihuahuas being greeted by two ladies wearing lots of make-up and jewellery, and stuffed into matching handbags with '*Gucci Poochie*' labels. I wondered if I'd see any of them again, and what adventures the dog-bowl-of-life would bring to my new life on 'The Reef'.

Chapter Two

An Out-of-Botty Experience

A warm breeze gently ruffled my fur as I stuck my head out of the taxi window. At first sniff Tenerife smelt, well ... smelly, and it definitely wasn't raining. Wooftastic! After the flight-from-hell things were looking up. I was so happy to be with my family again, and so intrigued by all the strange new smells, that the journey raced past without me noticing the lack of grass, mud, and cows. Pretty soon we arrived at some place called 'Costa del Scorchio' and my new home.

The house was smaller than the old one in England and there was no garden, just a small tiled area outside. So, was that where I was supposed to do my business then? Anyway, wadever - no worries ... I was back with my family again, and these questions could wait until there was something in my stomach worth coming out the other end (or as us dogs say, having an "Out-of-Botty Experience"). I went for a sniff around to see if I could find my dog bowl.

Sharon put this red plastic bowl-like-thing on the kitchen floor and said: "don't worry Gizmo, your bowl is coming with the rest of our stuff on Monday. It just needs to stay at customs for a few days". So what's that all about then? Haven't these customs dudes got dog bowls of their own? Why do they need to borrow mine? I don't remember giving my permission to loan it out. Blooming cheek! Oh well, I 'spose I'll just have to put up with this plastic tat for the moment. In fact it was a real pain-in-the-mutt's-butt trying to eat out of it. Every time I put my snout in to grab some food, it slid away from me across the tiles. Pure comedy. Now I knew what the humans meant by a 'dog's dinner'.

As I was trying to grab some food from this excuse-for-a-bowl, a small brown creature emerged from a little hole in the wall and made a dash for it right across my food. Before I could snaffle it, the slippery little bugger disappeared under a kitchen cupboard. A piercing scream interrupted my munching. "Blimey what's happening folks - has the roof fallen in? I've got a dog's dinner to finish here". Sharon was standing on a chair, pointing to where 'Speedy Gonzales' (the little brown bug) had disappeared. A few of Speedy's mates peeked out from below another cupboard (probably to see what all the commotion was about), setting off more screams.

I must admit, they weren't particularly pretty critters (maybe that's why Sharon was shouting something about "cocks" and "roaches"), but were they really worth all this fuss?

I mean, it's not as if they're some kind of alien life form ... or maybe they were? Note to self: wait till you've sussed them out further before attempting to chew on one. Not that I could catch one anyway, but I might have some fun trying.

Trev came rushing into the house and started dashing around trying to catch Speedy and his mates. The tiles were slippery and Trev was sweaty, so the chase was quite an amusing spectator sport for me and Sharon. After about ten minutes he gave up and started spraying this disgusting toxic chemical everywhere. We all had to leave the house.

The humans went out to eat and left me on the terrace. I hadn't even had a chance to finish my dinner, and here I was being abandoned again. Woof-Bloody-Tastic! Eventually they rolled back at about one in the morning, making quite a racket, and rudely waking me from a very entertaining dream involving rescuing some rather fine bitches from an army of little brown alien critters. Apparently my humans had made some new friends and "had a few drinks". I wondered if my new life in paradise would be quite as idyllic as my first impressions had promised.

The next morning started late as Sharon and Trev were feeling a bit 'ruff', but once they'd dragged themselves out of bed we all went out for a walk. "About time too" I was thinking, but us dogs are stoic. We don't complain much, and anyway I was excited to have my first chance to explore the neighbourhood. As we strolled around Costa del Scorchio I couldn't help noticing how many bars there were. Must be a lot of thirsty people around. Some of the bars had a sort of loud wailing noise coming from inside, which was apparently called: 'karaoke'. To me it sounded like a Chihuahua with a firework stuck up its bottom, but apparently some humans enjoyed it. Weird eh?

Just then a local pooch moseyed on up, giving me the chance to say "hola" in my best Spanish Woof. He gave me a funny look and replied: "hi mate, well here's a ting ... I don't speak de Spanish lingo". It turned out he was actually Irish. He told me his name was Clooney, and he went on to explain that his master owned one of the karaoke bars: 'Los Wailing Leprechauns'. Apparently the local Canario mutts were quite fluent in English Woof, so he'd never really needed to learn Spanish. He'd tried to speak a bit when he first moved out, but then never had the chance to practise. He invited me to join him in his master's bar that evening and enjoy "the feckin marvellous oi-didilly karaoke singing". I politely declined, saying that I had a previous engagement listening to a couple of cat-dudes scream at each other on my neighbour's wall. He gave me a funny look, shrugged, and wandered off.

Trev popped into one of the big hotels to ask if they had any work for him (he's a chef). From the look on his face when he came out he wasn't successful, but he told us not to worry, there were plenty of other places to try and "something's bound to come up". We wandered around Scorchio exploring hotels, bars and shops, while I grabbed the opportunity to start marking out my territory (an arduous and lengthy project for any 'new dog on the block'). Anyway, nothing did come up for Trev, so we went home.

That night things didn't really improve. Sharon was still upset about "them 'orrible cockies". The spray hadn't killed them all, and she found a survivor climbing up her leg while she was sitting on the toilet. After that she spent most of the night in tears saying she "'ated it 'ere" and wanted to get on the next plane home. Tracey joined in, and started balling her eyes out as well. I thought about having a good howl myself. After all, I was really missing my dog bowl, and there was probably some other pesky pooch with his nose in it right now down at this customs place. Trev calmed us all down, and told us that "we 'ave to make a go of it 'ere, cos like, it's a new start an all that".

The next few days passed without incident until Monday arrived. Customs were due to deliver all the rest of our stuff, including my bowl, in the morning (yeah right, don't hold your breath!). We waited all morning for the lorry to arrive, had lunch, and then waited some more. It finally arrived at 5pm. Trev tried to ask the delivery man what had happened? Why hadn't they turned up when they said they would? Why hadn't they phoned? But he just shrugged and kept saying "que?" as if it was entirely normal to be at least five hours late ... which for him it was.

We were beginning to realize that things worked differently here. If something arrived some time on the day it was supposed to, then that was actually an efficient delivery service, never mind how many hours you'd had to stay in waiting - that's irrelevant. Some people call this the 'mañana culture', but in fact it goes much deeper than that. It's actually more like a whole alternative universe: the 'Mañana Universe' (MU) with its own unique laws and principles.

For instance, built in to the way things worked in this MU universe was the (relative) certainty that everybody would be late for an appointment. The game was guessing by just how much (the so-called 'Mañana Uncertainty Principle' - or 'MUPpet's Law'). If someone were actually to turn up on time, the delicate balance which is the 'Mañana Space-Time-Continuum' would be thrown into complete mayhem, nothing would work, and the entire universe might even be sucked into a black hole created by an on-time delivery man.

I think I've already mentioned that I'm a highly intelligent super-sophisto dog, and understand these kind of things. So I knew there was actually a whole branch of quantum physics devoted to studying how things work in the MU universe. A good example of this was the washing machine in our new home. It was a kind of 'mañana washing machine'. You switched it on, and it made helpful noises for while, but then it would sort of shrug and go for a siesta, and you'd be left wondering if perhaps it would decide to finish the rest of the spin-cycle some time in the indefinite future - perhaps when the sun had gone down and all the other washing machines had sprung into life for a bit of 'electrodomesticos socialising'. The mañana washing machine always knew if it was a fiesta day. There seemed to be one of those most weeks, and no-one / nothing worked. Again the game was predicting when they'd occur. MUPpet's Law seemed to have something to do with it, because there was certainly a lot of uncertainty involved in guessing when a fiesta (or the washing machine) would spring into life.

We'd been here barely a week, and we were already finding out that things were hardly ever quite as they initially seemed in this new universe. For one thing, some things could be both true and untrue at the same time, without much of a contradiction, or anyone actually being accused of being economical with the truth. The locals had a phrase that you'd hear quite often: "mas o menos" and there were others: "temporary problem" meant "could take an unlimited number of mañanas", and "no problem" equalled "time to get really worried".

Another source of uncertainty in the Mañana Universe was that most of the time, things that *could* go wrong *did* inevitably go wrong, but sometimes they'd surprise you by working - if not perfectly, then at least a hell of a lot better than you'd ever thought they would. English-speaking humans have expressions that express the first part of this: Sod's Law, Murphy's Law ... the French say stuff like "c'est la vie", and as we dogs say: "Life's a Bitch". But the dogs around here say: "Mañana's a Bitch ... preferably a hot poodle with a cute little butt!"

Anyway, I digress. Fascinating as this stuff is, let's get back to our story. When the lorry did eventually arrive, lots of boxes were unloaded and I had a sniff around to see which one my dog bowl was in. Predictably one box had gone missing, and with the sickening inevitably of The Law of Sods, it was of course the one with all my stuff: dog bowl, bed and toys. Blooming feckin typical!

The delivery hombre said: "no problemo, it no have nada important in it". Yeah right señor Fur Brains, you're barking up the wrong tree matey, now I really have a bone to pick with you. I started making my growling noises. I think they make me sound dead macho, but judging from the reaction I usually get, I think I need to work on them a bit more so they sound less like a knackered vacuum cleaner starting up. Trev looked at me and said: "maybe we can claim on the insurance". Too right we will! But Sharon said: "come off it Trev, Gizmo's stuff ain't worth worth the 'assle." Excuse moi, but my stuff is worth quite a lot to me actually! After that I decided to lay low and sulk for the next few days, while the humans tried to sort out all *their* stuff (lucky them), along with the jungle of paperwork that they needed to live in Tenerife.

Paperwork here certainly involved a lot of work as well as mountains of paper, and even I had to have some. Apparently I needed a local dog license to prove that I actually existed*.

Of course nobody else bothered with this bit of paper, but my humans wanted to start off on the right foot, so Sharon decided to visit the paperwork office in Costa del Scorchio. Most people know the score and are fully prepared to wile away a few hours there. They bring supplies: food, water, books with at least 600 pages, sleeping bags ... you get my drift. Of course this was Sharon's first expedition to the office, so she arrived woefully unprepared.

She joined the queue to get a ticket with a number that specified her place in the main queue. Eventually she was given ticket number six thousand and eighteen. After about an hour and a half spent gazing at the counter as it slowly ticked off the numbers, 6018 was called, and she sat down at a desk to explain the situation:

"Sorry, I don't speak Spanish, but I've been told that I need a license for my dog, Gizmo. I've brought my passport, and I've even got one for him. Look here's his picture - isn't he gorgeous?".

There was no reaction from the stoney-faced woman behind the desk. From Sharon's perspective she may as well

* "I Woof therefore I am" does the trick for me, but we'll leave that thought for later.

have been talking to a robot. She looked at Sharon's documents, shook her head slowly, and finally said something:

"Señora, it is necessary the photo copies from your dog's pasaporte".

Sharon had spent the past ninety minutes becoming very familiar with the well equipped office, and had noticed the rows of photocopying machines all lit-up and ready to spring into action, so she wasn't too fazed by this request:

"Well that shouldn't be too much of a problem, can't you photocopy it for me?".

There was a pregnant pause, a moment of tension and this-does-not-compute. The robot (señorita GrumpyBot) slowly raised her head and stared at Sharon with shock and disbelief. Sharon might as well have asked her to switch off her power supply and re-boot herself.

"No es possible! it is necessary you go to the shop. You get there the photo copies." A hint of a smile flitted across the robotic features as she helpfully added: "you no need copy all the pages - only pages with informations".

Sharon was not amused: "but I've just queued up for an hour and a half" she spluttered.

GrumpyBot stared at Sharon blankly, shrugged, and said nothing. Sharon knew that she'd lost this particular battle, so she got up and went to get the copies done.

Fifteen minutes later she was was back in the paperwork office. Again she queued for a ticket, waited a couple more hours, and prayed that she wouldn't get Ms GrumpyBot again. The other officials behind the desks also looked like robots, but much friendlier models. Of course Sod's Law came into play, as it always does in this situation, and you guessed it ... her number was called, and she reluctantly sat down at the same desk and produced the photocopies of Gizmo's passport. GrumpyBot shuffled through the papers, and again the hint of a smile flickered.

"You no have pages ten, eleven, and twelve. It is necessary copies of these pages as well".

Sharon glared at the robot and replied: "but you told me to only copy the pages with information on".

She paused to allow the robot to savour her moment of triumph, and then it was her turn to smile ... "anyway, luckily I did copy all the pages, so that's OK then!". She passed the missing pages to the stoney-faced robot.

Ms GrumpyBot reluctantly continued with the procedure: "it is necessary I ask you some questions. Please to tell me the first names of your grand parents, your cousins, and is your dog having any little Gizmos?".

Sharon replied with the first names that came into her head: "OK no problem - Gertrude, William, Tony, and Gizmo is definitely not a papa. He's had the snip".

"I no understand this snip ..." but the information was entered into the computer, and Sharon was given six pieces of paper each of which she had to sign three times. After about fifteen more minutes of manic typing, and some violent stapling of all the various bits of paper, Sharon was handed the license with a flourish.

"Yeehaa, result!" she thought to herself, but her joy was short lived - apparently this piece of paper was only a temporary license.

GrumpyBot explained: "someone from the office is calling to you the next week, and it is necessary you come back here for the official document. Unfortunately I am on holidays, so no here, but one of my colleagues is giving you the paper".

Sharon shuddered at the thought of another visit to the office, but she was relieved that she wouldn't have to deal with Ms GrumpyBot again: "thank God for small mercies she thought" as she finally left the office exhausted, starving, and dehydrated.

It was the same story for all the rest of the paperwork. You needed the correct bits of paper to be allowed to exist (in my case) or to earn your living (for my humans), but getting the right paperwork didn't leave much time to look for real work.

Trev eventually found a job in a Hotel, but the wages were crap, and what little savings we had were being eaten up fast. So Sharon started working part-time as a cleaner. What little money she earned was cash-in-hand, and she was part of the 'black economy' - no holidays, no health cover, no sickness benefits or pension credits. So it was cash in hand, and hand in pocket to keep me in dog biscuits. I noticed that they had started giving me 'El Cheapo' dog food which was playing havoc with my digestion, but they still managed to find enough dosh to go out drinking and buy cigarettes.

Once they were both working they didn't have as much time to take me for walks, and they both seemed to be tired all the time. Tracey wasn't much better as she was more interested in playing with her new friends, rather than spending time with me. Forget the wall-to-wall sunshine, and having lots of 'quality time' to enjoy outdoors - now I was stuck in the house all day. I started to get a bit bored with my 'new life' in 'paradise', and began to develop 'Compulsive Chewing Disorder'. Shoes, biros, sunglasses, books, watches - I didn't really care what I chewed as long I could get it into my mouth and alter its shape in an interesting way, or even better, completely destroy it. Sharon and Trev weren't too pleased about this, especially when they had to take me to the vet after several of their prized possessions disappeared into my stomach.

Tracey noticed the problem first. One day we were enjoying a rare play session, when she shrieked: "Gizmo's got something growing out of his bottom!". I must admit I had been having real problems. However much I ate, and however hard I pushed, nothing was coming out of my rear end. So off to the vet we went.

When we arrived at the surgery and sat down in the waiting room, there were a couple of worried-looking cat-dudes in cages (let me at 'em) and a maniacally yapping poodle jumping up and down on her owner's knee. I soon realized why they were so worked-up as I turned my head and made eye contact with a massive slobbering Rottweiler, who was already sizing me up for his next meal. Perhaps he was there to get a few more tattoos.

"Hang on a minute" I thought, "I recognise that ugly mutt". Surely it had to be Rambo, the Rottie with the 'fur of flying' who liked dressing up in frilly outfits.

"Hola Rambo, how's things mate? remember me? we met on the plane".

Rambo snarled back: "you speakin to me you mixed breed mutt? If you breathe a word of what I said on the flight, I'm not going to be happy. So make my day punk - comprende?"

"Sure, sure, no worries" I stuttered in reply.

"Rambo's a pussycat really", said his owner. Well sure, I knew that, but the rest of the waiting room were all thinking: "yeah right, we believe you ... NOT!". The cats in the cages were praying to The Great-Moggie-in-the-Sky that they wouldn't be Rambo's next snack, and the poodle was now clinging for dear life to her owner's neck. Not content with merely scaring the shit out of us (not that it was working in my case), Rambo started shaking his head making his jowls wobble quite disgustingly, and we all had to duck to avoid his projectile slobber - hmmm, nice! Luckily it was soon my turn to see Miguel (the vet) and escape from Rambo's warm embraces and bad breath.

Miguel lifted me up onto the table and Sharon explained that I had problems doing my poo. He started examining my tongue, but she said: "no no, it's Gizmo's rear end that's the problem". Perhaps he was just trying to delay the inevitable pleasure of inspecting my cute butt, and I suppose I couldn't really blame him. Anyway, he donned the glove, applied the lube, and began to explore where the sun don't shine. There was indeed something stuck up there causing a blockage. Quite a few things actually: bits of twig, string, slippers, gardening implements ... you name it, it was all up there. God knows how - I didn't remember eating half of that stuff.

With a resigned look and practised dexterity, Miguel managed to clear the blockage. Wow, what a wooftastic relief! Talk about an out-of-botty experience, but it was only short-lived. A thermometer was rapidly inserted where the detritus had just been extracted (as if I hadn't suffered enough humiliation). Miguel was concerned that I might have torn something inside and have an infection, so he needed to take my temperature. Happily it was normal, so I got a biscuit, a pat on the head, and that was that (at least until I found some more tasty looking sharp objects to chomp on).

Things started to go downhill rapidly in the Gizmo household. Trev was sacked when he refused to do loads more work for the same money. They actually wanted him to come in two hours early and cook for four hundred more guests. Even a dog can work out there's something not right about that, they were, as Trev said: "aving a larf". Then Sharon's hours were cut, so very little cash was coming in, and the strain began to show. They were arguing all the time, and the rent hadn't been paid for two months.

One day the landlord banged on the door and told us that he wanted us out in two days, or else he'd call in the heavies. Sharon just snapped and booked a flight back to the UK with her credit card, but she only had enough money for two tickets. So she and Tracey were going to go back first, and Trev would follow later. That night the family started packing.

Wait a minute, I don't think I heard my name mentioned. I was going to need a ticket and some injections before I could go back to the UK. Tracey soon realized that I'd been left out of their plans, and told them that there was no way she was leaving me behind (bless her) but Sharon reassured her: "don't worry about Gizmo, daddy will sort out a flight for him as well". Phew, that's a relief then - or so I thought ...

The next morning Sharon and Tracey left for the airport. They each gave me a hug and said they'd see me again soon. Trev stayed with me all that day, which was great. He took me for three walks and gave me an enormous meal - real meat not the dried stuff. I slept really well that night cos I was stuffed with food, and tired from the walks.

The next morning when I woke up Trev wasn't there. I thought that he'd probably just popped out to get some milk or something. So I went back to sleep, but when I woke up again he still hadn't come back. I was really desperate to have a pee by now, so I had to relieve myself in a corner of the living room. I hoped that Trev wouldn't be too angry with me when he came back, but I just had to have a pee or else my bladder would burst!

Darkness fell and Trev still hadn't returned, so I started barking. Perhaps someone would hear and let me out for a pee. So I woofed and woofed, but all I got was the neighbour banging on the wall and shouting: "shut the fuck up!". Eventually I got too tired to bark any more, and fell asleep.

The next morning there was still no sign of Trev. I began to get quite worried. What the feck had happened to him? What if he'd had an accident? The house was smelling bad by now - I had to go to the toilet somewhere. Even more worryingly, my water bowl was now dry. I tried barking again, but my throat was sore from all the woofing I'd done yesterday, and I was so thirsty. One of the windows was slightly ajar and I tried to open it, but it wouldn't budge and I couldn't even squeeze my paw through the gap. By the afternoon I was feeling quite ill, and I fell into a fitful sleep.

Some time later I was woken by the sound of the door being opened. "Yee-ha Wooftastic! Trev's come back for me". But no, he hadn't. It was the landlord and a couple more big hairy humans. When they saw me, they all started shouting and the landlord rushed towards me waving his arms violently. I thought it was probably a good time to leave, so with my last bit of energy I made a dash for it out of the front door.

Chapter Three

Mean Streets

I ran as fast as my paws could carry me, and my heart was beating like there was no tomorrow. There was no looking back at the house. Now I knew for sure that they'd buggered off and left me, and I was on my own on the mean streets of Costa del Scorchio. Eventually I stopped running, and it hit me like a ton of the smelly stuff hitting a fan. I really was on my own. No-one was going to feed me, or hug me, or call me a good boy. Now I was a street mutt, a stray, an abandoned dog. Just one of the many that wandered the streets of Tenerife. That was that my furry lad. From now on: no more pampered pooch - time to get street-wise. Yep, as we dogs say: "life's a bitch", but we're stoic when things like this happen. We've got very strong survival instincts, and we just get on with making the best of a bad situation.

My quick getaway had left me panting and my mouth dry. I hadn't had a drink since yesterday afternoon, and I was desperately thirsty. I had to find some water, but it wasn't that easy here. It hardly ever rained, so there were no convenient puddles to drink from. I thought I'd try one of the bars. Maybe someone would give me some water. But no, they just shooed me away and told me to go back home. They didn't understand: I didn't have a home anymore! My owners got on a flight, fecked off back to England, and left me to fend for myself. All I wanted was a drink of water - not too much to ask, surely?

Then out of the corner of my eye I saw a man cleaning the pavement with a hose. Wooftastic! I dashed to the water, and lapped it up as quickly as I could. Soon I was joined by other stray mutts, all of us slurping and slobbering for Tenerife. The spray man was yelling angrily at us, but I was allright now. I wasn't thirsty anymore, so I ran off.

The next urgent problem was the the rumbling and gurgling in my tummy. I hadn't eaten for more than twenty-four hours, and my stomach was demanding that this be rectified. I had a sudden brain-wave: let's go and check out my Irish amigo Clooney at 'Los Wailing Leprechauns'. He might have some food.

Clooney was sitting outside the bar looking depressed. There was none of the usual wailing coming from inside. The Leprechauns must have all buggered off.

"What's up mi furry amigo?"

Clooney sighed. "Oh mate, it's feckin bad. The boss had to close the bar cos he's run up such bad debts and we're going back to Ireland. I've had all my injections and we're going this evening! They had a whip-round last week to pay for my flight. So at least there's no way he's going to leave me behind".

I was sad that he was leaving. I could have done with a friend like him right then, but I was glad that he wasn't being abandoned like me. He couldn't believe it when I told him that my no-good humans had done just that. He was very sympathetic:

"I'm so sorry to hear about your feckin eejit family Gizmo. Best of luck mate. You'll be fine, you're one smart woofer ... not like those stoopid eejit excuses-for-dogs that come round here in handbags. Now dem guys I'd be well worried about if they were dumped on the streets". We said our good-byes and wished each other the "hair of the dog".

I wandered off, rummaged around some bins and discovered a half-eaten hamburger with mustard. Not bad, quite tasty in fact. I knew that the mustard would probably upset my stomach, but hey as they say: "beggars can't be choosers" and I was definitely a beggar now. I felt a bit better after I'd eaten, so I went for a little trot around the harbour. I met a lady taking her pooch for a stroll. She came up to me and looked to see if I had a collar with a phone number, but of course Trev had made sure that he'd taken it off. She patted me on the head, and said that I looked like "such a cute doggie - how could anyone abandon you?".

"Yeah too right" I thought.

Her pooch gave me a sniff and woofed: "really sorry amigo, bad luck, but my mistress can only afford to look after one of us". I told him that I wouldn't eat much, and I just needed somewhere safe to sleep. I gave the lady the cutest look I could muster, but she seemed so upset that I walked away. I didn't want to make her feel bad, and I could see that she really couldn't help me. l found a place to sleep and dozed off.

Some time later I woke up to find a cute little Caniche sniffing me out. I made for her rear-end to introduce myself with some serious butt sniffing, but the wooferette came over all coy and skipped off down the street. What's that all about then? I thought she wanted to say hello, but obviously not. Bitches, I don't know, sometimes I just dog-gone don't get them! Anyway, wadever ... I wandered off in the opposite direction.

A few minutes later I heard a woofing frenzy. Looking back, I saw this big ugly mutt barking aggressively at the little poochette whose cute butt I'd just tried to sniff. I thought: "hmm ... shall I join in? haven't had a good woof for a while". So I trotted back down the street to join them. When I arrived on the scene, Ugly Mutt was baring his teeth and creeping ever nearer to the Caniche, who by now was shaking with fear.

I was angry. If there's one thing really gets up my snout, it's big ugly mutts picking on smaller pooches - especially cute little lady pooches. It's not fair and it's not right. Plus I'm a real sucker for whimpering chicks. They can really twist me round their paws when they start crying. So I prayed to the Big Dog* in the Sky and charged in, woofing very loudly.

Ugly Mutt turned to find the source of this rude interruption, and while he was distracted the damsel-in-distress made a speedy get-away. He gave me his best bully-boy snarl and charged at me. Up close and personal he was even bigger, meaner, and smellier than I'd imagined.

"Hmm ... maybe this wasn't such a good idea!".

So I did what any sensible pooch would do in the circumstances: run like crazy. When in doubt, a dog's danglies are always worth preserving. Fortunately before Ugly Mutt could react (for all his snarl and slobber, fast reactions were not his forte), I heard this little old lady yell: "Buttercup, stop that and come here immediately". I kid you not, that was actually Bully-Boy's name! My snarly-slobbery amigo Rambo would have approved, and maybe recommended an anger management course.

Having narrowly escaped having my mutt's nuts clamped in Buttercup's jaws, I wandered off towards the beach, and who should I see there but the cute little damsel-in-distress. She introduced herself as Katy, apologised for her earlier flighty behaviour, and thanked me gratefully for coming to her rescue. Of course she hadn't actually seen my hasty retreat from the Jaws of Death, and I wasn't about to spoil the image she had of me as her hero. Some things are best kept on a need-to-know basis, don't you think?

(* by the way, isn't it interesting that humans have never figured out that what they call 'God' is actually a Big Backwards Dog)

Katy explained that she'd also recently become a stray. Her humans had been forced to leave their house in a hurry (now where have I heard that before), and move to a tiny apartment where no dogs were allowed. So one evening they drove to a car-park in Costa del Scorchio, opened the car door and just dumped her on the street. She told me that she'd stayed in that car-park for at least four days waiting for them to return. Of course as I've already explained, us dogs see time differently. So for her, those four days all merged into one very long moment of waiting. Anyway, her owners never came back for her. She was probably only about six months old - just a pup; really sad, and all on her own.

Us woofers do wonder about you humans sometimes. We think to ourselves: how can you do some of the things you do? I mean, I know dogs can be pretty cruel to each other, but for us it's 'dog eat dog' (sometimes literally). You humans are supposed to be above us animals aren't you? I didn't want to think about it too much, my head was spinning and my stomach was rumbling again. I needed to find some food, so I said adios to Katy and went in search of my next meal.

I only got a few metres before I heard a pathetic little whimper. Of course now that I was her big hero, she was upset that I was leaving. Never mind that she was first with the butt-sniffing, and then got all sniffy herself when I'd tried to return the compliment. But like I said, bitches can really twist me round their little paws when they start making with the whimpering noises. I'm a big-hearted pooch. A real softy in fact, and I can't bear to see a bitch cry. OK I thought, it might be good to have some company for a while, so I said she could tag along. But I warned her, before she got too many romantic ideas about 'us', that I wasn't too big on responsibility. After all, I was only one-and-a-half years old myself, and I wanted time to play the field a bit before I settled down with pups of my own. And anyhow she was just a pup herself. So, we were just amigos. "OK, wadever ..." she said, licking my nose and cuddling up to me. I wondered if she'd really got the message, but I have to admit she felt good next to me.

The way things turned out, teaming up with Katy wasn't such a bad idea. My new amiga was a cute little fluffy white Caniche-style pooch, a bit of a 'mini-me' in fact. As I've mentioned, I'm actually a Lab-Doodle - a rather handsome mix of the best bits of a Labrador and a Poodle. So neither of us were anybody's Poodle, and both of us were pretty good looking dogs (even if we did need a bit of a groom by then). We made a great team when we went scrounging for scraps from the restaurants. A bit like human beggars who have a baby with them, people liked the fact that we were a cute little family. Especially when we put on the hard-done-by looks. To be honest it wasn't too difficult to do a hard-done-by look, because hey, we *were* hard done by!

We'd often hang around the cafes and bars in calle Vomito on the infamous 'Hurlo strip' in the late morning, when they were serving the full English breakfasts. The tourists who ate in these places were called '*gambas*' (prawns) by the locals because of their two-tone pink-white complexions.

They usually sported a few tattoos, a pint of larger, and were often on the chunky side of life. Let's put it this way: sitting under one of their chairs would be to take my life in my paws and risk being squashed as it collapsed under the enormous weight. Saying that, as long as we managed to avoid death-by-squashing, these tourist humans were certainly generous, and we used to get quite an assortment of food thrown to us, before the waiters would shoo us away.

Wandering the streets all day and night we came across a lot of cats, and I have to say that in my humble opinion, cats are pants! I'm sorry but I've got to get this off my chest. They really pee me off. They trot around acting all superior, looking like they own wherever they happen to be perched, and they're teasers of the worst kind. For example, typical catty behaviour is to sit on a high wall lording it, and waiting for an unfortunate dog to pass below. Then they smirk as they watch the poor pooch go crazy, barking and leaping manically.

Meanwhile they're giving him that knowing look. Know what I mean? The look that's been passed down from generation to generation of smug pussies. The look that says: "na-na-n-na-na ... you can't get me ... I'm far too high-&-mighty for a miserable mutt like you to reach". Then when the exhausted woofer finally collapses in a heap on the ground panting for his life, the moggy jumps off the wall and strolls down the road, nose in the air, knowing that the poor pooch hasn't got any energy left to chase them. These feckin feline felons can be so cruel they're positively evil!

There were other pests that made life on the mean streets a pain. Along with not having a home, or anyone to give you a regular meal and a safe place to rest your paws, there were those pesky fleas. They know a free ride when they see one. For them, a stray mutt is an opportunity for some property speculation. They size up the most 'sought after' woofers, and then they just move in to your fur. They do it without your permission. It's not like they're giving you any rent, or contributing anything to your up-keep. They're just squatters really, and once they've moved in they're bloody difficult to evict. These annoying little critters were really driving me nuts. The little buggers were keeping me up scratching all night, and I was getting almost no kip.

I was also starting to get a bit worried about Katy. She'd had a bad case of the runs for the last few days and seemed very lethargic. I must admit, my digestive system wasn't functioning much better either. It wasn't surprising really, most of our food was scrounged from the bins or left-overs that people would chuck us. Admittedly the fried food was tasty, but the tourists' diet was doing us no favours.

We decided to leave Costa del Scorchio and explore a bit further afield. We walked along the coast for quite a way until we came to a bustling fishing village called 'El Blowo' (apparently this was short for: 'El Blowo-de-Sombrero-Offo"). It looked like a cool place. Feckin windy that's for sure. Almost blew my fur off in fact, so maybe it would blow a few of those pesky fleas away.

We stopped outside a cafe on the board-walk called 'Flashpoint'. They'd left a bowl of water on their steps just for passing pooches. How considerate was that - wooftastic in fact. I was starting to like this place, and we decided to stick around for a while.

Some of the humans there were wearing rather strange outfits. Skin-tight black rubber gear which smelt well weird. Actually the more we sniffed it, the more we liked it. Apparently they were called 'wet suits' and some humans wore them to go in the sea. Judging from the odour, these suits were also handy when they were 'caught short'. Hmm - nice, I approve.

The real purpose of these smelly suits was to keep the humans warm while they were doing some funny stuff called 'water sports' (after all, the poor things didn't have fur coats to keep them warm, like we did). Apparently El Blowo was famous for water sports like surfing, windsurfing and kite-surfing because the non-stop wind made the sea very bumpy. Funny eh? That would just make me sea-sick, but these humans-in-smelly-suits liked to use the bumps to leap into the air. They called it: "getting some air" ... ironic really, cos for us dogs this means passing wind and sniffing it - far more logical (and pleasurable) really.

Water sports were certainly peculiar activities to spend your life doing. The participants had to carry all this heavy equipment across a sand-blasted beach, chuck it in the water, and jump on. Then they spent several hours charging around, getting their air, and falling off. It looked daft to me, and I'm not even sure that I'd call it a sport. I mean, where was the ball? or the stick? or the frisbee? Humans can be such strange creatures sometimes.

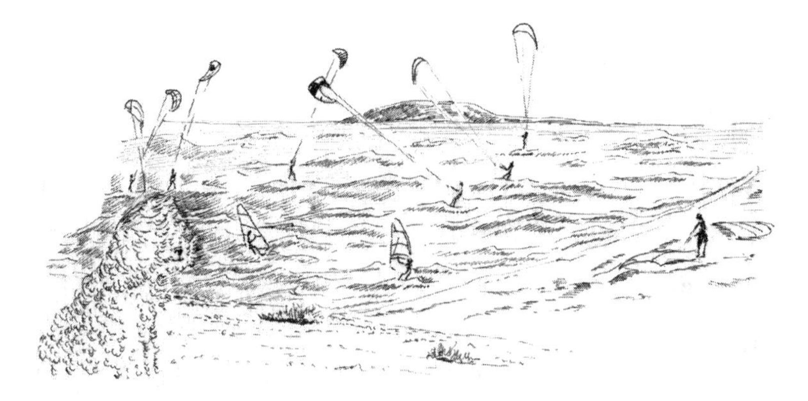

We spent quite a while in El Blowo, checking out the restaurants (well their rubbish bins anyway), and getting to know some of the local pooches. One of them was a cross-breed mutt called Stitch. She had a cool life as the official cockroach catcher for a local surf station, but spent most of her days snoozing outside the door, and sniffing new customers as they came in to hire equipment. She only had to fulfil the roach-catching duties on a part-time basis, and anyway it was fun work chasing those little brown buggers around. Most days the surfy customers would throw a ball for her to chase on the beach, but Stitch said she was a bit tired of that ...

"What do they think I am? a performing Poodle?". I knew what she meant. Of course, as I've explained, I'm more street Doodle than swanky Poodle, but neither of us were *anybody's* Poodle. We were very much our own dogs. She was a bohemian surf dudess, and I liked to think of myself as a sort of 'working-class hero', standing up for the Under-Dog, even if it did get me into a fair few scrapes on the mean streets of The Reef.

Katy and I also used to hang out with the local Yorkshire Terriers. You couldn't avoid them really, they were everywhere in El Blowo. We spent some time 'bone picking' about life with four of them: Nacho, Paco, Hugo and Conchita. They all had homes, but they were happy to have a woof with us strays while their humans sat gossiping on a bench in the Plaza. I asked them why there were so many Yorkshire Terriers in the town. Hugo explained: "it's because us Yorkie dudes are such babe magnets, and well ... a woof's as good as a wink, know what I mean? say no more!".

I wasn't very convinced by this answer. It was laughable really, especially given that Hugo was well passed his 'babe magnet' days. In fact he was probably already entitled to his free bus pass, but I didn't want to argue with him. Yorkies can turn quite nasty if pushed. They're like mini-Rottweilers in a terrier disguise. So I changed the subject.

Anyway, as I said, we woofed about a whole variety of things, but Conchita got a bit bored when we discussed anything remotely serious. She'd start inspecting her paws, primping and preening, and generally getting peed-off that she wasn't the centre of our attention. To be honest, I don't think she had too many brain cells. A bit of a fur bimbo in fact, but she soon perked up when Katy asked her which groomer she went to. Then we couldn't get her to shut up!

I felt sorry for Katy. She was a pretty little pooch, but her fur was starting to look a bit ratty. No brush had been near it for a quite a while, and until she found a new home there wouldn't be much chance to visit any of the fancy groomers

that Conchita kept woofing about. Never mind though, at least in El Blowo she could always pass it off as a fine example of the 'surfy look', which would always be popular there with so much wind around.

I might have stayed longer in El Blowo but disaster struck. I was parted from my amiga Katy. We'd just finished off someone's discarded pizza, and were wandering down towards the beach. Katy went ahead for a pee behind a rock, and just as she finished a van drew up beside her, and two men dressed in official looking uniforms got out. I didn't like the look of these guys so I woofed at Katy to run, but she was paralysed with fear and just stood there shaking. The men trapped Katy in a net and bundled her into the van. It was the feckin dog catchers!

I ran towards the van as fast as I could, but it was too late. They were already speeding off into the distance. Eventually I stopped running when I couldn't see the van anymore, and lay down on the pavement panting heavily. My little amiga had been taken away, and I was alone again. Waves of sadness swept through me. I missed her already. I hadn't realized how much I'd got used to waking up next to her, and having a soul-mate to share my thoughts with.

I decided to leave El Blowo. I really liked the town, and we'd had some good times there, but now there were too many sad feelings drifting around the place. So I said my adios to Stitch and the three hundred Yorkies that lived in El Blowo, and wandered off towards the hills. I'd heard that there were lots of dogs living up there in big houses, surrounded by fields, called '*fincas*'. Maybe someone on a finca could give me a home. After all, they should have plenty of space for me, and the grass would surely be greener up there.

Chapter Four

Fighting for Life

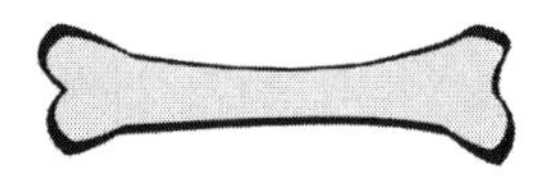

I set off up the hill out of El Blowo heading for the mountains, clear air, and new adventures. Perhaps there was a new home for me up there. Maybe up among the trees that I could see way in the distance. Hopefully I'd find someone to look after me. Maybe there'd even be fields and mud and stuff. So I trudged on, onwards and upwards, until I came to a dusty farm track leading off towards some fincas.

When we come to cross-roads like this in our lives, we have to take a decision: do I take this path into the unknown, or stay on the well-trodden highway? OK, what the hell, I decided to chance my luck with whatever was down the track. Actually, being a dog, the decision wasn't so existentially tricky as the track smelt the better option: intriguingly rural, with some kind of exotic animal dung, and a faint aroma of food lurking in the distance.

I'd got a fair way into the countryside when I saw this small human coming towards me. He seemed friendly, and he had a piece of cake in his hand, but for some reason my canine instincts told me not to trust him, and I started to back away. He kept talking to me softly, and then he opened his rucksack and brought out a salami. That did it. I hadn't eaten in three days and the smell of the salami was overwhelming. I sidled up to him and grabbed the salami from his hand. He let me munch it for a while, and then he slipped a rope around my neck. To be honest, I was so relieved to be eating at last, that I wasn't too bothered.

When I'd finished eating, he led me down the track to a run-down old farmhouse surrounded by several beaten-up outhouses. There were rusting old trucks with cactuses growing in them, and a smell of decay everywhere, but hey it had to be better than sleeping on the street. I thought: "this ain't too bad. Maybe I've fallen on my paws this time, and I'll be living with a family again". But the bad-vibe doggie instincts kept creeping back into my mind, despite my dogged determination to ignore them.

As we came closer to the farmhouse, I could hear barking coming from one of the outhouses. "Wooftastic, I won't be an only dog here. But hang on ... those woofers don't sound very happy to meet me." Nope, it definitely wasn't full-of-joy, excited-that-someone-new-has-arrived woofing. They should have been telling me: "this is our home, and we're in charge here. We guard the place for the boss, but hey we haven't got a bone to pick with you. Let's have a look at you, and if we like what we see we may even give you a friendly lick." Nope, this woofing was nothing like that at all. It was a woof of desperation, of dogs who haven't been let out to play. It was a we're-bored-out-of-our-minds woofing. These dogs were prisoners!

There was a shout from inside: "Miguel, where the hell have you been? have you found another mutt for us?"

Panic hit me. Time to get out of here. I pulled on the rope around my neck and tried to slip out of it, but it was too tight and the little boy (Miguel) had a firm grip. He dragged me through the back door of the house and into the kitchen.

There were four men seated around the table drinking and talking loudly. These guys were a bit how-can-I-put-this: 'ruff and ready'. They all had tattoos and the sort of stubbly hair that humans grow when they want to look 'well 'ard'. Their clothes had seen better days - like some time the previous century, and the air was a heady mix of garlic, tobacco, alcohol and sweat. Actually their whiff was the only thing that I liked about them.

At the head of the table was an extra mean-looking small hombre (yet again the villain is the little guy. It's always the same: Hitler, Stalin, The Poisoned Dwarf ... all vertically challenged. OK, I made up the last little chap, but you get the picture). He seemed to be the boss of this motley crew. As we came through the door he jumped up, glared at us menacingly, and shouted angrily at Miguel: "what the fuck are you doing with this dog? He's no use to us. Look at him! How many times have I told you - we need ugly, fierce dogs. What are we going to do with this pathetic runt? He's some kind of fucking Poodle!".

I was thinking: "hey, now hang on señor Fur-for-Brains, "pathetic runt" is one thing, but I'm nobody's feckin *Poodle!* (as I've already explained, I'm a Doodle). As you guys have noticed, I'm definitely not ugly, and I'm not particularly fierce (although by now I was starting to feel ready for some serious snarling). I obviously don't fit the job description, and I don't recall answering any ad that said: "Wanted: Ugly Fierce Dogs for Exciting New Opportunity". So now we've got that straight, maybe your son can untie me and I'll leave your house with the greatest of pleasure."

Unfortunately Miguel choose that moment to put his spoke in: "papa I really like this one. He looks so sweet. Can't I just keep him in my room?".

The other guys around the table fell about laughing at this. Miguel's father (the mean-looking stunted hombre) scratched his stubble for a moment, then said to his son: "OK, come to think of it, it might be good to have a pretty dog in the ring for a change. Maybe that would bring the punters back".

This seemed to upset Miguel, and he pleaded with his father: "no Papa, please, not this dog! He won't last two minutes in the ring. I'm really sorry I brought him back. It's my fault, I won't do it again. I can take him back to where I found him, and just let him go."

"Sounds like a very sensible suggestion" I thought, "cos this ring place doesn't sound too friendly to me".

Miguel started to undo the rope, and I was just about to make my escape, but his father grabbed me by the scruff off my neck and dragged me out to the sheds where all the woofing was coming from. Miguel was crying and pleading with his father to let me go, but all he got in return was a vicious slap around the head. This hombre sure was one mean bastard, and from then on I decided to call him: 'El Bastardo'.

He opened the door of the shed and shoved me inside. As my eyes adjusted to the dim light, the sight that met me was horrific. Rows and rows of cages full of dogs, all chained up. So these mutts were chained up, locked in cages, inside a dark stinking shed ... just as I'd thought: these poor pooches were prisoners. My fur froze with fear, and I did something I hadn't done since I was a pup, I wet myself. This didn't go down too well with El Bastardo. He aimed a kick at my head and threw me into one of the cages. There was just one other dog in there - an ancient Pit-bull. He was covered in scars, and looked like he'd been in plenty of scrapes and seen better days.

Now, obviously a Pit-bull wouldn't have been my first choice of kennel-mate, and to put it mildly I was shitting myself (again something I tried not to do since my puppy days). I got ready for the inevitable submissive roll-over, but as I looked into this old warrior's eyes, I realized that there was no need to worry. There was no fight left in the old boy. His expression was one of hopeless despair, rather than aggression. I didn't need to woof with him to know that he just wanted to be left alone.

I curled up in the far corner of the cage and hid my head, which was still throbbing from El Bastardo's kick. The din of desperate woofing had calmed down when this nasty little man slammed the shed door shut. There was just the sound of whimpering, snuffling and snoring as most of the dogs fitfully slept.

Some time later I was woken up by a sort of doggie hissing sound, and to my amazement discovered that the mutt in the cage across from me was none other than my old mucka from the aeroplane: Rambo! (You remember him: the Rottweiler with the 'fur of flying' and a closet pink-frilly-outfit wearer). He might not have topped my list of acquaintances to share this hell-hole with, but having listened to his confession on the flight, I knew that he was a fellow traveller. I felt like shit, but at least there was now an audience for my rather individual 'humour'.

"Hey amigo, fancy meeting you here. It's a small world eh? There again, I know you like to hang out in all the trendiest spots".

Rambo woofed back: "yeah, right Gizmo, very funny ... Not!".

I asked him what on earth he was doing here?

"Well, my owner was short of cash, so he decided to sell me for fighting and he brought me up here. I've been locked up in here for ages. I haven't had a fight yet, but I'm shitting myself just thinking about it. I may look tough, but you know me Gizmo, I'm really just a big pussy-cat."

"Umm, yes, not really ... not too many cats can slobber quite like you mate, but I know what you mean" I thought.

"I only pretended to be fierce to please my owner. It's all bark and no bite with me. Last night El Bastardo tried to get me to attack this other dog, but all I could manage was a bit of barking and spitting. He beat me with his belt, but I still couldn't do the fighting, so I just lay on the ground until he stopped"

I wasn't liking what I was hearing, but Rambo carried on woofing and it got worse ...

"Our cages only get cleaned once a week. Just look at the filthy mess we're in. The only excercise we're allowed is the fight training. He starves us, and keeps us chained up, then he puts us in the ring with a rabbit or a cat, and expects us to pull it to pieces. The chains are suppose to build up our muscles so we fight better, but all it's doing for me is making me weak."

"Feckin 'ell, I'm in deep doodies here" I thought. "Now I understand the stuff about me not being ugly or fierce, and why that kid wanted to keep me out of the ring". Rambo wasn't finished yet though, he'd saved the worst for last:

"I just want it to be over Gizmo. The best way is to let yourself be killed in a fight, cos unless you're bloody good at it, fighting back will only prolong your stay in this hell-hole. Anyway, even the champion dogs don't get treated much better."

I got the message now: "Woof-Bloody-Tastic, so we're between a rock and a very hard place here. Give in and get torn to pieces, or fight back and you live to fight again - if you can call it a life."

Rambo was in full flow, slobbering and snarling now: "it's not a life! Every day's the same - pain, pain and more pain. It's not even a dog's life, we barely exist! That poor mutt in your cage fought back, and just look at the state *he's* in."

Bruno, the Pit-bull, lifted his head wearily, turned to look at us and said: "listen to Rambo - he's right. A pooch like you Gizmo, you haven't got a hope in hell amigo. In the beginning I thought that my owners would come and rescue me, but now I know they're not coming. I don't think they even know where I am."

I asked Bruno how he'd ended up in El Bastardo's shed. "I was stolen from my back garden when my owners were out shopping. Just 'cos I'm a Pit-bull, El Bastardo thought I'd be good in the ring. So he came up to the back gate and threw me some meat. Then before I knew what was going on, him and his mates put a sack over my head and I was chucked in the back of their van. For a while I did what they wanted and fought back in the ring. I thought it would buy some time for my owner to find me. But now I know I'm on my own. I've been bitten half to death in that ring. I'm exhausted. I've given up now. It's all over for me."

So, as the politicians like to say: we were all in the deep doodies together. No way out. A wave of deep depression washed over me and like Bruno, I just felt done in.

"I'm going to sleep now Gizmo. It's the only pleasure I've got left. Maybe I can dream about my old life, when humans loved me. My family used to take me for long walks. They gave me hugs and I even slept in the same bedroom as them. We were hardly ever apart."

He sighed: "happy memories - that's all I've got left now. That's all any of us have in this hell-hole. Buenas noches mi amigo." He flopped back into his corner of the cage and we both fell into a fitful sleep.

I was woken up a few hours later as the door of our cage was opened. Bruno was being lifted out. El Bastardo shouted to his partner in crime: "get your arse in here, we've got a dead one to chuck out, and he's fuckin 'eavy."

I licked Bruno's nose before he was hauled out. At least his pain was over now. He was out of this hell and away to a better place where all dogs run free. His story was so sad. If his owners hadn't gone out that day he'd still be with his family, enjoying a life that every woofer deserves. You know - where the humans actually take care of us and love us, instead of hating us.

"Rest in peace my furry amigo. I'll be seeing you soon. I won't survive long here either."

El Bastardo turned his attention to me. "Well now my pretty Poodly one, you can have the cage all to yourself now. Enjoy it while you can. Your turn for fun-and-games soon!"

The days passed in a haze of loneliness, hunger, and pain. I didn't talk to Rambo anymore. My fur was caked with dirt and I started to smell pretty bad. Normally smelly is no problemo for us dogs, but this was way beyond acceptable. After all, they wouldn't let me out of the cage to do my business and they only cleaned it once a week.

Miguel gave me scraps of food occasionally, when El Bastardo was out looking for more dogs to kidnap. He always cried when he saw me. I felt sorry for the kid. It wasn't really his fault that I was in here. He'd wanted me as an amigo, to care for and play with. Poor kid didn't have much joy in his life either, with a bully like El Bastardo for a father.

We didn't see much of his mother. She used to wander around aimlessly with her head bowed, never saying anything. Sometimes she'd have a black eye or bruises on her face. I was pretty sure she was also on the receiving end of El Bastardo's fist.

I really don't understand you humans sometimes. I mean, how can you do stuff like that to your own family? Humans often call other humans 'animals' when they're talking about their bad behaviour. They say things like: "that so-and-so is a real *animal* - he broke his wife's nose just cos she burnt his dinner". But you know, us *actual* animals would never be cruel to our pups or partner. In the animal world, we're always very protective of them.

One day both doors of our prison were opened and I saw daylight for the first time in ages. El Bastardo and his cronies put ropes round our necks and led us outside. I could barely walk I was so weak. The weeks in that cage had drained my strength and my will to live. A large van drove into the yard, and we were stuffed in the back. We drove along bumpy tracks for ages, and eventually arrived at a bar somewhere up in the hills. It was cold and dark. I could hear a lot of drunken men shouting, and the sound of dogs fighting. The humans shoved us into more cages, and left us alone.

"So this is it" I thought. The end had come. It was all over. It's funny how your life flashes past at times like this. I thought about the good times ... when I arrived as a pup at my new home; the walks, chasing cats, the tasty treats, playing ball on the beach, and sharing time with Katy on the street. I really hoped that she'd found a good home. "It hasn't been such a bad life, eh?" I thought, but I could have done with it going on a bit longer.

My thoughts were cut short as rough hands grabbed me and threw me into the ring. There was a lot of laughter at my entrance, and the audience were calling bets on how long I'd last before I was torn to shreds.

"What odds do I get on a minute? Reckon he'll last that long?" someone shouted.

I was praying that it wouldn't take that long as I waited, frozen with fear, for my 'opponent'. Finally the dog that was going to end my life was led into the ring. Yep it was one mean brute of a Rottweiler, all snarls and slobber. I looked up at my executioner, and I couldn't believe my eyes ... it was Rambo! We gazed at each other dumbstruck.

"Mate I can't fight you", he whispered.

"Rambo, you have to. You've got no choice. Either you fight me, or they'll just kill both of us anyway. Look, don't worry, I'm ready to die."

"No no, mate, I just can't do it - you're an amigo, and anyway you know I'm not a fighter."

Out of the corner of my eye I could see El Bastardo starting to move towards us.

"Come on Rambo. Just go for it. El Bastardo is getting angry. Get it over quickly for my sake, please.'"

"OK" said Rambo.

I closed my eyes waiting for the first bite, and the searing pain, but all I could feel was a lick on my face.

"Rambo, mate, this isn't going to work. You've just got to attack me."

"Gizmo, I don't care. He can beat me to death, but I'm standing my ground. I'm not going to do it. Not all Rottweilers are killing machines".

"Wow, he's one brave pooch!" I thought.

There was a lot of disappointed shouting from the punters. This was not what they'd come to see. El Bastardo strode into the ring, undid his belt, and started beating Rambo. I couldn't look, and curled up in a ball.

Then something else. Another twist. Between Rambo's agonised woofs and the crowds' mocking shouts, there was the sound of a siren. A black van screeched to a halt. Men in uniforms jumped out and were grabbing hold of the drunken audience.

I looked over to Rambo. El Bastardo had stopped beating him now, and was edging towards the exit.

I woofed to Rambo: "lets go, this is our chance to escape."

El Bastardo saw us making our get-away and rushed towards us. I felt a searing pain as his belt come down on my back, but Rambo, my hero, went straight for his trousers. He grabbed him by the leg, and I managed to make a run for it.

I looked back once to see where Rambo was, but he'd disappeared into the night.

Chapter Five
Friends Re-united

I ran through the blackness of the night, not daring to turn my head. If I was being pursued I didn't want to know. All that mattered was to get away from El Bastardo and his prison. I hoped against hope that Rambo had also managed to get away from that terrible man, and that our paths would cross again, hopefully in happier circumstances. So I ran and ran until finally I dropped, exhausted, near a low stone wall somewhere in the countryside, and fell asleep.

I must have slept deeply, because when I woke up the next morning there was a human talking to me softly. My first thought was "oh no, he's found me!" and a rush of panic hit. I tried to get up on my paws and attempt to run, but I was so weak that I fell straight back down again. Yet again I was at the mercy of another human. I looked up at the new tormenter's face staring down at me, and I couldn't believe my eyes. I recognised that face - it was Trev!

He looked quite different though. His hair was longer and very matted, and he had more hair on his face. His clothes were dirty, and he smelt rather 'interesting' (as we dogs say). Generally he looked a bit 'ruff', just like me in fact. But I didn't care. I licked his face enthusiastically, just not believing my luck. It was so good to be with my master again. Trev gazed down at me, and tears started rolling down his face.

"I don't deserve you Gizmo. After I pissed off and left you, and you can still give me the time of day."

The thing is: us dogs don't really hold grudges. Most of the time we're stoic. We accept what life throws at us - the good, the bad, and the ugly (which is just how we were both looking right then), and we don't really complain. For sure I wouldn't be so overjoyed to see El Bastardo again, but Trev was OK(ish). After all, despite how things had ended, we'd had some good times together.

He picked me up gently and started walking, with me in his arms. It felt wonderful to have someone hold me like that again, with so much love and affection. Tingles of joy raced through my fur. I did my 'floppy thing' in his arms, and kept licking his face. He carried me to an empty finca where he'd been staying, and as he carried me along, he kept talking to me softly:

"I can't believe you're here with me Gizmo. It's a sign. My luck's changed, now I need to change as well. I can see that now, and you'll see too Gizmo. I hit rock bottom. We both have, but this time I promise things will be different. If you just give me another chance, I'll do right by you this time. Just you wait and see."

I let him talk while I kept licking. To be honest, I didn't really care about the past. Everybody deserves a second chance, and I was just so happy to have someone looking after me again. After all, a dog without a master is like:

- toast without butter
- fish without chips
- cappuccino without the frothy stuff on the top
- or a large planet without gravity ... because, of course, if you decided to jump in the air (for a squeaky ball for example), without gravity both the squeaky ball and you would just float off into space. So, you get my drift (woof woof :-)

Anyhow, when we got to the finca Trev gave me some tasty morsels to eat, and started to fill up an old iron bath with water from a hose. I must admit (and I don't often admit to this) it felt great to be having a bath. Finally I could kiss good-bye to those pesky fleas that had been squatting in my fur, rent-free. After the bath he gave me the rest of the salami, and I realized that he'd just given me the last of his food, and his only meal for the day.

He wiped me down with an old t-shirt, and we sat together while my fur dried in the morning sunshine. He stroked my head and kept talking to me softly: "I'm so sorry that I left you in the apartment Gizmo. It was a terrible thing to do, but I wasn't thinking straight. I knew that we had to get out of there before the landlord chucked us out and took all our stuff, but I only had just enough money to send Sharon and Tracey back home. So I lied to them that you and me would be joining them in a few days."

"Aha, so now the truth is coming out" I thought.

"My credit card was on the limit, and after I bought their tickets I couldn't use it anymore. I didn't tell them, but a mate had been loaning us the money to carry on. I already owed him thousands, so I couldn't ask for more money to get you and me back to the UK. In the rush to get them home and us out of the apartment, I sort-of forgot about you. Well, I 'spose the real truth is that I blocked you out of my mind. Now I can see what a terrible thing I did."

He was sobbing quietly with his head in his hands, but he desperately wanted to finish the story ...

"I've screwed up badly, my furry friend. I've let you and my family down. The dream life in Tenerife just didn't work out as we planned. It turned into more of a nightmare really! OK, so I didn't like my job in the UK, but at least it was regular work with a regular wage, and I could provide for my family. When the hotel sacked me cos I wouldn't take a pay cut, it was the beginning of our downward spiral. I lost all my confidence, and it was impossible to find another job. All the restaurants and hotels are cutting back on staff. Not speaking Spanish didn't help either."

"I've been lying to Sharon and Tracey, telling them that I'd found another job and I was saving up for my plane ticket, and yours as well. Every time they ask about you I feel so bad. I'm sure they can hear it in my voice, but I've been dreading telling them the truth about how I abandoned you. Then they want to know why I haven't booked a flight yet ... but the truth is Gizmo, I've been living on the streets like you. I'm so ashamed and I'm so sorry."

I licked away the salty tears pouring down his face, and it seemed to cheer him up a bit.

"When I left you behind in the apartment, I thought that the landlord would be bound to feel sorry for you and take you to the dog refuge. I didn't have the guts to do it myself, and I couldn't face telling Sharon and Tracey. So like I said, I just blocked you out of my mind."

"It was a terrible thing to do - you could have starved to death in that apartment. Since that day I've been having nightmares about it, wishing that I could turn back the clock."

I looked up at Trev, and saw real sorrow and remorse in his face. I put my paw on his arm, as if to say: "it's OK mate, I understand, we all make mistakes in life. What matters is admitting that we made them, and learning from it. That's what makes us wiser."

For instance, this reminds me of a hard lesson that I've had to learn about cats. I know I said that cats are "pants", but now I think that was wrong. It was a mistake to think that we could simply chase all the pesky critters right off the planet. It's just not possible, and actually it's not even healthy for us dogs to declare war. Chasing them is wooftastic sport - yes, but tearing them limb-from-limb is just not acceptable these days. Though it pains me to say it: we do have to live together in relative harmony.

So I admit I made a mistake, and now I've moved on. Enlightened dogs like me don't go in for catist hatred any more, and we don't agree with catism. Generally, the kind of dog that is still openly catist isn't my kind of an amigo anyway. They tend to be all bark and no bite, all snarl and slobber, but when you cut to the chase they're usually far too fat to catch up with even the laziest pussy. OK, I'm not saying that I'd necessarily want to share my last bone with a cat. I'm not even saying stuff that I've heard from other dogs like: "some of my best friends are cats" (yeah, right), but I'm reminded of a quote from that great canine philosopher, Snoopy:

"Sometimes when I get up in the morning, I feel very peculiar. I feel like I've just got to bite a cat! I feel like if I don't bite a cat before sundown, I'll go crazy! But then I just take a deep breath and forget about it. That's what is known as real maturity."

And to that, I'd just add: 'real wisdom'. I always try to keep this in mind when I see one of them feckin moggies sneering down at me from the neighbour's wall.

Anyhow, I digress ... Trev's mood changed when I put my paw on his arm. He seemed to understand what it meant. He laughed ruefully, and his voice changed: "honestly Gizmo, anyone would think that you can really understand everything I've been saying."

Well scratch my bollox - had he only just realized? we *did* understand each other! Of course we did. Maybe not in the conventional human way, with words, but he certainly understood the point of my paw gesture, and I understood what he'd been telling me - from the music of his voice, the looks into my eyes, and his tears. We were communicating perfectly, with emotions rather than words.

It's funny really. On the one hand humans don't think us woofers can understand a word they're saying, but then on the other hand they expect us to come running as soon as they call our names; or not to lick that tasty morsel of horse shit when they tell us what it will do to our stomachs. We can chew bones but not their slippers, and when they explain this they expect us to understand and obey.

Ha, I seem to remember that Trev even used to talk to me about his problems with Sharon. "I'm in the dog house again" he'd say to me, as he took me for my morning walk. "'Er Indoors is giving me grief again", and he'd go on about it for the next fifteen minutes, when all I really wanted was for him to let me off the lead and throw a ball for me to chase. But never mind, apparently I'm a Man's Best Friend, so I'll listen to his tales of woe about 'Er Indoors, but they really should make up their minds about this, and decide whether we can understand their lingo or not.

Of course your average family pooch isn't bothered about any of this. Basically he'll just suit himself, and only really respond to commands when he feels like it, or when biscuits are involved. However, I'm a bit different. I think I've already mentioned that I'm a highly intelligent super-sophisto woofer. When it comes to understanding difficult stuff like this, I'm the mutt's nuts, the dog's danglies. So, as I've explained, I can communicate directly using state-of-the-art canine communications: gestures, sounds, smells and emotions.

Trev looked at me, and he seemed to have come to a decision. "So, as you can see my furry mate, right now all I have are the clothes on my back and not much else. You and I both know how lonely it gets on the streets, and I'd love to give you a home, but right now there's nowhere that I can call home."

"Oh no, I can feel where this going. Not again ..." I thought.

"I don't want you to suffer any more than you already have Gizmo. You look like you've really been through the wars my poor pooch." Little did he know how true that was!

"Those wounds look like they're infected - you're going to need some medical treatment, but I haven't got any money to pay for it. You need a proper home, with someone who can give you the care and attention you deserve. Not me. Right now I have nothing. It wouldn't be fair on you."

Just as I thought: this was deja vu and Groundhog Day all over again.

"Look Giz, I know a really good refuge where you'll be well looked after until they can find you another family. It's going to break my heart to say good-bye again, but take it from me, this time it really is for the best."

I had to admit, he had a point. Not that I was looking forward to this 'refuge', whatever that was. I just hoped that it wasn't anything like El Bastardo's shed. But as I keep telling you: us dogs are nothing if not stoic, plus all this talk about a new home with a new family had made me nostalgic for the creature comforts that I'd once enjoyed.

So Trev and I walked to the refuge. It took us a few hours, but it was good to be walking beside a human again. As we walked along the dusty track he spoke softly to me, talking about the good times we'd had back in muddy old England, and how happy I'd be with my "new family". I did my stoic, resigned best and tried to stay optimistic. This was going to be a fresh start, and hey whatever else it would bring, there'd bound to be more adventures.

My story has certainly had a fair few twists and turns along the way. Who'd have thought that I would have just bumped into Trev like that, and here we were, taking this twisty track together to goodness-knows-where. I'd survived so far, partly through good fortune, but also on my wits. Hey, I was a street-wise woofer now, and I was almost starting to enjoy the unpredictable adventures that it brought. At least life hadn't been dull since leaving the creature comforts behind. Yes, I was going to miss Trev (again!), but you never know what was waiting just around that corner ... "hopefully a nice juicy steak" I thought.

When we got to the refuge we were greeted by the manager: Marta. Trev explained the situation to her: "this is Gizmo. He's a very special dog, and he needs a good home. Please, please can you take him in? I've heard so many good things about your refuge. The dogs get the care and medical attention they need, and then you try and find a good home for them. Look at me. I just can't look after Giz properly any more, so I'm begging you, please take him."

Marta checked to see how many dogs were in the refuge and said: "OK, you're in luck. I do have a place for Gizmo. I'll take him, but you've got to understand that once you leave him with us, that's it - he's not your dog anymore."

Trev looked sad, but he replied stoically, almost doggedly: "I understand. That's the way it's got to be. Just look after him well, OK?"

Marta looked me up and down, and said: "he's a really sweet dog. Like you say, quite special in fact. I don't think it'll be too long before he finds a home. Once he's had a good wash, we've got rid of all his fleas, and he's had time to recover from his sores, he'll be very presentable."

I was thinking: "'ang on a minute, I had a bath yesterday. How many baths can one dog have, before he smells sweet enough for these feckin female humans?".

Trev knelt down beside me and and spoke to me softly, with tears in his eyes: "good-bye Giz, my cute furry friend. I'm so sorry that it had to end like this, but like Marta said, you're one special doggie and someone's bound to fall in love with you very soon, just like I did. Adios Gizmo I'll never forget you"

He gave me a last hug, then he stood up and I watched him walk slowly away. He didn't turn back to look at me, just carried on walking through the refuge gates and into the distance. Yet again I was being abandoned, and I felt the familiar rush of desperate sadness and panic. I tugged at my lead and tried to follow him.

Marta kept a firm hold of me, knelt down and whispered softly in my ear: "hey, don't worry Gizmo. You'll be fine. I'll put you in a cage with some other friendly dogs to keep you company. So cheer up, it's dinnertime soon, you must be hungry."

Now, I know I'd been having fantasies about a nice juicy steak, but funnily enough, after Trev walked away and left me there even the thought of food couldn't cheer me up. I'd known in advance that he was going to leave me in the refuge of course, but when it happened for real I felt the familiar feelings flood through me: loneliness and emptiness. Once again though, it wasn't long before the stoicism and survival instincts that are part of us dogs' genes kicked in again. Hey, sheet happens (quite a lot to me it seemed) and then we move on.

Marta's vet gave me the once-over and I had some flea and tick treatment. My fur was trimmed and my various wounds were treated. Then she put me in a cage with a few other mutts. My new home was thankfully nothing like El Bastardo's shed. It was actually quite spacious - for a cage anyway. We could even wander outside to do our business and have a bit of a nosey around. So, more like a real home - or at least a 'sought after' cage.

I must admit though, that first night I didn't get too much sleep. Well none of us did really. My cage-mates were: Gonzales - a manic Jack Russell (we called him "Speedy G") and Luna, the Bulldog. Speedy G kept bouncing around all night like he thought he was some kind of manic rubber ball. He bounced off the walls, me, Luna, everything really! and in between bounces, he insisted on telling me his life story - in great detail. Then when Speedy G's battery finally ran down and he decided to go to sleep, Luna started snoring for Tenerife. Crikey, what a racket! The planes flying low over the refuge were nothing compared to Luna's snoring. Maybe that was why she'd found herself on the streets - perhaps she drove her owners completely mad with sleep deprivation.

The next morning the nice people at the refuge gave me some breakfast. Wooftastic! What a treat after having to ferret around for food on the streets. It almost made up for the lack of sleep. Then one of the volunteers took me for a walk. Aha, now things were really looking up ... that's until I got back to the cage to find yet another woofer had appeared. So now there were four of us in there, and it was getting a little bit cramped. "Not much chance of moving pad and getting some kip now, they must be full" I thought. Oh well, sigh ... not wanting to start off on the wrong paw with the new arrival, I greeted him with a welcoming sniff.

The new mutt was Elvis - some sort of a Terrier / Spaniel mix. He seemed friendly enough, until he started making this weird noise. It sounded a bit like a pig trying to sing karaoke while being strangled. I thought: "hang on mate, I know it's quite a privilege to meet a pooch of my calibre, but calm down please!". Unfortunately there was no stopping him. The strangled-pig karaoke wailing continued on-and-off for the rest of that day and night.

So there I was, stuck in a cage with a woofer who thought he was a rubber ball and bored the fur off me with his cat chasing stories; a mutt who snored louder than a Boeing 707; and now, a pooch who thought he was auditioning for the doggie version of X Factor ... Woof-Bloody-Tastic!

I'd been at the refuge for a few days, more-or-less (as I say, us dogs aren't too bothered about time), when the dog catchers brought in a Chihuahua. She was making a hell of a racket with her screechy little woofs, and I prayed that she wouldn't be joining us in our cage. I'd only just got used to Luna's snoring, Speedy G's manic bouncing, and Elvis' wailing, but you guessed it: mini pain-in-the-butt mutt was stuck in there with us. Funnily enough it turned out I knew her. It was Fifi, one of the Chihuahuas on the Flying Fur flight. I said woof to her and sniffed butt.

"Get orf my hind quarters you mangy mutt" she squeaked.

"Charming!" I thought, "I bet you don't even remember me, and by-the-way your 'quarters' didn't smell that wonderful anyway".

"I'll have you know, I'm a Chihuahua don't-you-know, and chav dogs do *not* get to sniff my anatomy."

"OK, calm down dear" I woofed back, "what are you doing here anyway?".

This seemed to get to her. "There's been a terrible mistake. I shouldn't be in this horrid place at all" she bleated.

"Its the same for all us chica" I replied. "None of us should be dumped in a refuge. We should all have a home, with a family."

Fifi spluttered: "but, but, but ..." ("OK dear, we're over the butt thing now, move on" I thought to myself). "I'm special. You cannot expect me to live in a place like this. I'm not used to slumming it like you street mutts".

"Well mi amiga, you better get used to it, at least until someone comes to adopt you."

"No, no, no ..." she wailed ("why the feck does she have to say everything three times?"). "My owner is coming to collect me very, very, very soon. Just as soon as she realizes where I am."

"Maybe she will, maybe she won't" I said gently.

She looked at me, paused for moment, and started a high pitched howl. It was as if someone had pumped her full of air and then released it through her 'hind quarters' like a squeaky balloon.

"That's just great!' I thought. "Just what I need right now. A new kind of ear-piercing racket to enjoy. Join the club - they'll love you."

I shoved a bowl of food underneath her nose. The horrendous squealing stopped abruptly, as if the balloon had burst. She looked down her nose at it, and said disgustedly: "what on earth is that?".

"Umm, duh, it's called dog food, don't-you-know".

"No, no, no ..." (here we go again, apparently only exclamations in triplicate are enough for this bitch) "you cannot be serious. I can only eat freshly cooked chicken with brown rice, smoked salmon, or occasionally caviar".

I humoured her: "well OK Fifi, I know you're more delicate than us rough chav mutts, but unless you eat this stuff you're going to get very hungry".

She thought about this for a second, and then reverted to her cloud-cookoo-land optimism: "I think I'll wait till my owner comes to collect me. I don't want to upset my stomach"

"OK mi amiga, suit yourself" I woofed, and strolled out of the cage into the play area to chase speedy G around for a while and sniff a few more friendly butts. When I returned to the cage Fifi was curled up in a little ball.

"Why hasn't my owner come for me yet?" she sniffed.

I was tempted to reply: "maybe cos she can't afford your food bill", but to be honest I was feeling a bit sorry for her now, even if she was a stuck-up bitch. As I think I've already mentioned, I'm a bit of a sucker for a chica in distress, so I woofed as gently as I could: "hey, she's probably looking for you right now, but if she doesn't find you, I'm sure that you'll get adopted by another Chihuahua lover really soon". Then I asked her how she came to be picked up by the dog catchers.

"Well I was at the hairdresser with my mistress. She was having her usual perm. When she was finished, she asked the hairdresser to look after me for a few minutes while she went to the cash machine. But then she never came back".

Fifi was starting to sniffle again, but she went on with her tragic story: "the hairdresser was really annoyed because my mistress hadn't paid for the perm. I heard her say that she hadn't paid her rent or bar bill for three months, and now she was expecting to get a free haircut. She was so angry that she got straight on the phone to the dog catchers to demand that they come and get me."

By now she was whimpering, and the full-on balloon squeals couldn't be far away. "My mistress isn't coming back for me is she Gizmo?" she wailed.

"I'm really sorry mi amiga, I doubt it, but like I said, you'll soon find someone just as nice, and maybe they'll be able to afford your diet".

I left her to sleep, crept over to Luna who was just starting to pump up the snoring volume, and woofed loudly in her ear. Hey, puppy-ish I know, but I just had to get my own back for all the sleepless nights. Luna woke up with a confused start, grunted and woofed: "what the dog crap is going on?". She gazed around for a minute, shrugged and fell asleep again. A few seconds later the jets overhead were once again drowned out by her industrial level, heavy-metal snores.

The dog pen next to ours housed the bigger dogs, and I got quite friendly with a Canarian Presa called Manuel. He helped me brush up on my Spanish woof, which helped pass the time in between eating and trying to sleep. Manuel explained to me that the best way to communicate with the local Canarian mutts was to woof loudly and quickly, wave my paws around a lot, slobber a bit, and when in doubt over a woof or its pronunciation, just to add an 'o' onto the end of it (as in 'el bastardo, woofo, stinko' etc). This seemed to work surprisingly well, and from then on I got to know a lot more of my furry amigos in the refuge.

Trev was right, it wasn't too bad there. OK, not as good as a proper home with a loving family and soft furnishings, but we were well taken care of. The volunteers came to take us out for walks most days, and even though some of my fellow cage-mates were a bit annoying, it was good to have company. Nope, things could definitely be worse (as I'd found out in El Bastardo's shed). All in all it wasn't such a bad life, at least as a temporary solution, but I did start to wonder about life outside the refuge fence. Some pooches had been in there for years (or at least they reckoned for a sizeable slab of time) and that was way too long for me. I hoped someone would give me a home and new adventures soon.

Chapter Six
A Very Special Dog

<FLASHBACK ...>

Basil the Yorkie had been ill for a while. His owners, Nikki and Richard were very worried about him. He'd spent most of his life in damp, muddy old England, but when he was nine years old they moved to Tenerife, and now they lived in El Blowo - the town with a thousand Yorkies. He felt quite at home there really, but he was getting on a bit. He still enjoyed his walks, woofing at the postman, and chasing the stray cats that dared to come into his garden, and he still kept up with his important role as The SpokesMutt for Tenerife-Dogs.com - a website run by Nikki to promote the refuges in Tenerife.

All in all, el Baz had lived a long and happy life (he was, after all, ninety years old in human terms) but sadly he was coming to the end of it now. He was fading away gradually, spending much more time sleeping, and when he was awake he was often confused - bumping into furniture, or just staring into the distance. So Nikki and Richard took him to the vet. The vet said that it might be a heart problem and prescribed some tablets. He told them to come back in a few days.

That night Basil's condition deteriorated rapidly. He'd always had these little fits, right from when he was a puppy. Perhaps it was something to do with in-breeding, but that evening it was almost as if a massive electric shock had ripped through his brain. He was shaking all night, and in the morning he couldn't walk. So Nikki and Richard took him back to the vet.

The vet was great. He wasn't overly sentimental, just very kind. He looked them straight in the eye and said: "if Basil was my own dog, I'd put him out of his pain now". It was clear that he would never recover or have any quality of life again, so the sad decision was made to put Basil to sleep. It was one of the most difficult things that Nikki and Richard ever had to do, but it was the right decision.

They spent the last few minutes of Basil's life gently stroking his head and saying adios to their furry amigo, as the injection was given to sedate him, and he gradually and peacefully went to sleep.

Nikki and Richard were devastated. El Baz had been such a big part of their life, now he was gone it felt empty. They went for long walks, wrote his

name in the sand and watched the sea wash it away. The grief was so intense that for a while they didn't want to get another dog. They didn't know if they'd ever be able to love another pooch as much, and they even worried that it might be disrespectful to his memory. He was an irreplaceable part of their little family, but they were 'doggie people' through-and-through, always would be, so deep down they knew they'd be adopting another pooch some time soon. Their lives would be a lot emptier till then.

<END FLASHBACK,
EDIT BACK TO GIZMO ...>

"Come on Gizmo. Get your paws moving. I know you love digging up the beach, but we've got to get you back to the refuge for dinner time". Karen, one of the hard-working volunteers who regularly gave up their spare time to walk the dogs, was having a bit of a hard time persuading Gizmo to leave his favourite spot.

Yeah well, who could blame me? Everyone loves the beach, no? It's fur-tastic fun digging a huge hole. I'm aiming for the world record, and who knows, one day I might just pop out the other side and say g'day to my furry mates Down Under.

But fair enough, I realize that there's more to a dog's life than digging, and I must admit I was getting a bit peckish. Karen bribed me with a biscuit, slipped my lead back on, and we walked back up the track to the refuge.

As we came in through the gate, I couldn't believe who was mincing around one of the other pens. It was none other than my old amigo Rambo - the Rottweiler hero who'd saved me from El Bastardo's clutches!

"Hola Rambo, so you made it, and here we are again. You just got here?"

Rambo looked at me about as warmly as a Rottie can manage, slobbered a bit, and replied: "no mate, I've been here for quite a while. I'm in the 'fierce dogs' cage over there by the office."

"Ha ha, that's a joke" I thought, "Rambo fierce? They obviously haven't seen him in his pink frilly outfit then".

He went on: "when the police raided El Bastardo's dog fighting ring, they bundled me into their van and brought me here. I've got a micro-chip but my owner's disappeared ... and thank feck for that, because I wouldn't want to go back to that bugger anyway. He didn't beat me or nuffin, but I didn't get much love, know what I mean? I think he only kept me to cultivate his 'ard man' image! To be honest I'm better off here. I've made some good mates, the humans aren't a bad bunch, and now my old amigo Gizmo's here ..." I think he almost had tears in his eyes, or would have except the slobber was in full flow.

"It's wooftastic to see you too Rambo", I woofed warmly.

We sniffed butt in a strictly manly (or rather doggedly male) way, and he carried on woofing: "I really hope they find me a better owner this time. You know, someone who likes to play with me, and gives me a cuddle sometimes. You know what a softie I am Gizmo".

"Yeah, well you may be a bit of softie Rambo, but you're one hell of a brave woofer. If it hadn't been for you I'd still be chained up in Bastardo's shed, or chewed up in little pieces in that ring. You saved my life Rambo, and I cross my paws that you find a good home now".

It was getting on for dinner time, so we woofed our good-byes, and I trudged back to my cage with its motley crew of inmates. Some important developments had occurred while I'd been away. Blooming feckin typical! When I turn my back for a minute, something interesting happens. Anyway, a human had actually agreed to adopt Luna. I hoped they had a good supply of ear plugs!

She gave me the low down : "yeah this old bloke came along and took me out of the cage this afternoon. He sat with me for a while, feeding me dog biscuits and patting me on the head. He seems really kind. He said he wanted to adopt an older dog cos he wasn't so quick on his feet anymore, and a puppy would be a bit too much for him."

"Yeah he sounds ideal for Luna" I thought "she's definitely no pup".

"He can't walk too far anymore, but you know Gizmo, that suits me just fine. I'm not that keen on this walking malarky, its very over-rated in my opinion." Then she came to the really important bit: "and guess what - Marta was talking to him, but he couldn't hear her cos he's stone deaf. So no problem with my snoring! Anyway he's coming to collect me tomorrow - she wrote it down for him".

Me and my canine cage-mates were happy for Luna, and relieved that we might finally get some sleep. Next day we bid her a fond farewell with a last butt sniff. I must admit I felt a little jealous. When was it going to be my turn?

That same afternoon a smart young couple with a small child took Fifi out of the cage and made a huge fuss over her. They'd been looking for a Chihuahua to adopt for ages, so she was in luck. Fifi was whisked away to her new home in a swanky new silver BMW. I think the car just about met with her approval.

Next to go were Speedy Gonzales and Elvis, in a two-for-the-price-of-one deal. They were both taken by another couple who owned a finca with lots of space - something they definitely both needed, and which was in short supply in the cage. So again I was happy for them, relieved that there'd be no more manic bouncing and wailing, but now I was also starting to feel a bit lonely and depressed. I really needed a home to call my own. When would it be *my* turn? How come all the other woofers in our cage had been adopted *except me*? Whenever a human looked at me in the cage they always said what a lovely dog I was. I just didn't understand. Maybe I was *too* pretty, could that be possible?

<FLASHBACK ...>

After Basil the Yorkie passed away, Nikki and Richard were devastated. They grieved for him and wondered if another dog could ever replace him, but there was such a big gap in their lives without a pooch that they started looking. It was tough. Every time they went to look at another mutt they found themselves comparing it to el Baz.

They had endless conversations about which breed they should get. Perhaps a Jack Russell - but they could be a bit too feisty; maybe a Spaniel - they sometimes had health issues. After their experiences with a pure breed they wondered whether a cross-breed mutt might have fewer problems. One thing they did ***know for sure - this time they would definitely be adopting a dog from a refuge and giving them a new home. There was certainly no shortage of candidates, the problem was finding one that they could both fall in love with as they had with Basil.***

A few weeks of fruitless searching passed, and they were starting to despair of ever finding a woofer

that would be worthy of the late great Baz. Then one day Nikki got a phone call from Marta ...

"Hi Nikki, I heard about Basil - I'm so sorry. Listen, I've got this very special dog here. He's about a year old, and a sort of mix of Labrador and Poodle. He's absolutely gorgeous. I'd have him myself, but I've already got Tio. You should definitely come and have a look at him before he gets snapped up."

Nikki said "OK Marta, thanks for telling us. We'll have to think about it. I'm still very upset after losing Basil, and I'm not sure if I'm quite ready for another dog in our life yet."

They talked about Marta's call and Richard's opinion was: "what have we got to lose? let's just go and have a look at him. If we like him we could just foster him for a few days and see how we get on. Let's just take it from there."

So Nikki called Marta back and agreed to come to the refuge that afternoon, and have a look at this *'very special dog'*.

<END FLASHBACK>

Chapter Seven
Wind of Change

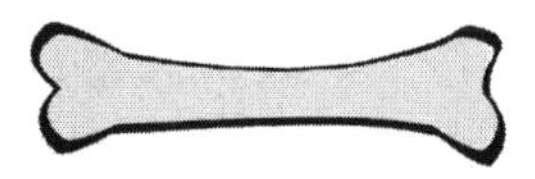

Time passed slowly for me at the refuge. Of course, as I've explained, us dogs can't tell how much actual time has passed, but it felt long enough. Some of this time I was alone in the cage, and sometimes other woofers joined me. Of course the refuge felt nothing like El Bastardo's shed. It definitely wasn't a prison, although we spent a lot of time 'behind bars'. We weren't treated like prisoners, but it wasn't exactly what I'd call a proper home either. It was more like a refugee / transit camp. A kind of limbo-land where we were all in a state of suspended animation - temporarily in limbo between humans that had abandoned us, and others that would hopefully give us a new home.

Life was OK, if a little predictable, but I could handle that. Us woofers like routine. A bit like Zen Buddhist monks in that respect. I was getting enough to eat (even if it was more menu del dia than cordon bleu); plenty of walks with the volunteers; and if I was lucky enough to get Karen then I'd get to do some running, swimming, and digging on the beach. I spent the rest of the time woofing with Rambo and dreaming of life outside the fence. Then one morning he tested my Zen-like stoicism to the limit by announcing that he too was about to experience life on the outside again ...

"Karen needs a guard dog for her finca, and she reckons that I'd be perfect."

I knew him well enough by now to risk a little sarcasm: "well yes mate you certainly look the part, and even if *we* know that you're really a bit of a softie, any intruder's going to skedaddle when he sees you in full-on slobber mode".

He ignored the slur on his Rottweiler credentials and carried on woofing: "she's already taken me up to her place to meet all the other animals. It's like a mini-farm with horses, chickens, cats, and quite a few other rescue woofers from the refuge. She was a bit worried that they might be fazed by me - being a Rottie, but no worries, after some serious butt-sniffing everything was cool."

It sounded idyllic to me - loads of space to run around and Karen even provided some critters to chase. Feelings of envy started to gnaw at my bowels (blimey, it must be dinnertime soon, surely?).

"Of course the chickens and cats are off-limit, but that's OK - I'm going to be part of a family again, and this time I know it's going to work out! Karen is so kind. She's a real doggie-person - gives me loads of hugs."

Well yes, I already knew that from our wooftastic walks on the beach. She would have been top of my own list in fact. So all this wasn't exactly helping my mood, but I tried to stay stoic for his sake.

"Her pooches told me that all we have to do is woof when someone comes near the finca. Well I think even I can manage a growl if it's some bugger who might harm my lovely mistress, eh Giz?". I agreed that the job description didn't seem too onerous.

"The rest of the time we can do what we want: eat, play, snooze on the sofa, anything except annoy the horses, bite the chickens, or chase the cats".

"Dress up occasionally?" I wondered, but kept the thought to myself and told him that I was very happy for him. It sounded like he'd really landed on his paws with Karen, and it couldn't happen to a nicer pooch, but when would it happen to me ? I must admit I was starting to get a bit depressed. It was enough to test even a Zen Buddhist's patience.

We woofed our farewells and sniffed butts in our doggedly male way one last time, but really I felt more like howling. He was more than just my best amigo - he'd saved my life after all! Deep down I knew that change is the only constant, and everything ends in the end, but little did I know that the wind of change was about to blow though my own life once again ....

One afternoon, not long after Rambo's departure, I was woken from my siesta by a very tall male human. He picked me up in his arms and gave me such a great smile that it felt impolite, in fact downright rude, not to give his face a good lick. Amazingly he didn't seem to mind at all (most humans find our slobbery behaviour a bit 'gross', but not the real doggie-people. It's a sure sign of one). He carried me to the office where a female human was waiting with Marta. When she saw me she exclaimed: "what a beautiful dog! What's his name?". Clearly this lovely lady had impeccable taste, but I tried not to get too excited. After all, other people had said stuff like that before, and here I was still stuck in my cage.

Marta said "meet Gizmo. He's been here a few weeks now and I think he's getting a bit lonely. All his mates have been adopted, but we've been waiting for the right people for him. He's a really *special* dog, but his previous owner just couldn't look after him properly, so he brought him here. Now he needs a good home."

I soon learnt that the couple were called Nikki and Richard. Apparently they'd only just recently lost their beloved pooch Basil, after 13 years. I thought: "wow If they adopt me, I'm in there for the long haul."

Marta explained that they could come back and collect me in a couple of days, and then look after me for a bit to see if we all got on together. I thought: "hey of course we'll get on together, I don't have any nasty habits ... well, not many anyway, unless you count the occasional fart. But hang on a minute, why wait? Why can't I leave right now?".

Apparently I needed to have an operation to stop me from having pups. All the rescue dogs had to have it. It was quite normal and the vet reckoned it might even help me to live longer. I have to say that I wasn't completely convinced: "hang on, just wait a dog-gone minute now. What bits of me are involved exactly? and will this affect my abilities in the impress-the-lady-dogs department? I mean, not to put too fine a point on it (ha, mine has never been that fine anyway - woof woof!) ... will I still be able to get it on with ma bitches?".

I woofed it through with some of the older more experienced woofers and they reassured me that the operation wouldn't be the premature end of my 'interaction' with the lady dogs. It just meant that I wouldn't 'be the daddy'. But hey, if that meant that I'd be getting a new human family, then so be it. Anyway, as I think I've already mentioned, having pups wasn't really on my radar. Too much responsibility for a dude like me. I needed to play the field a bit - know what I mean? So bring it on.

After the op I woke up feeling sleepy and a bit sore. I had to wear one of those ridiculous plastic lamp-shade things to stop me licking the missing bits. If humans were forced to walk around with a bloody great lamp-shade stuck round their heads, then maybe they'd understand how humiliating it feels. Anyway wadever ... as usual I was stoic about such things, and I soon cheered up when Nikki and Richard picked me up from the refuge the very next day.

I got into the back of their car and Nikki sat beside me stroking my fur. Wooftastic - not a bad start! They'd brought me a new lead and a soft blanket to lie on and I already had the feeling that these guys really understood us woofers. We soon arrived at Nikki and Richard's pad, and I had a good sniff around the living room. There were a few toys on the floor (grrreat - I love squeakies), and in the corner there was a well posh dog bed. This was getting better and better, and then I saw it ... the piece de resistance ... and my heart did a little dance. On the floor sat a beautifully crafted ceramic dog bowl! Now, you know how I feel about cheapo plastic bowls, but not this one. Oh no, indeedy-weedy, these people had taste. No rubbish plastic tat for Gizmo from now on. I looked at it in awe, then I noticed the bits of fresh chicken mixed with dog food in it. That's when it occurred to me that maybe this time I had really landed on my paws.

It was fantastic that they'd bought all this stuff for me, but I had a few more things to check out before I could feel well and truly at home. I jumped up on the sofa, and then went upstairs to the bedroom and leapt on their bed. No objections from my new humans, phew that was a good sign. I didn't want them thinking *they* ruled the house after all! So I thought I'd have a bit of a snooze on their bed and see what happened. No worries! Nikki just gave me hug and said that I was probably feeling a bit tired after my operation and all the day's excitement, and they just left me to sleep.

Because Nikki and Richard had only just recently lost their beloved pooch, Marta had said I was on 'probation'. They wanted to see how we got on together, and whether we bonded. But I could tell from the look in their eyes, and the huge smiles they gave me whenever I walked up to them for a cuddle, that I wasn't going anywhere. This was my home now. Yep, I think I could safely say that I'd finally landed on my paws. That night I slept soundly in my own posh new bed in the corner of their bedroom.

The first morning in my new home was wooftastic. I opened my eyes, jumped on their bed, and gave them a wake-up lick. A few polite woofs persuaded Richard to get out of bed, put a collar and lead on, and take me for a walk. So he was a doddle to train, but I soon discovered that Nikki didn't *do* mornings. Even if I did the Rumba round the bed, and recited key passages from "Dog Training for Dummies", she was not going to move. At least not before what she called a 'civilized hour'. But hey, no worries - she took me for my evening walks, played chase-the-squeaky, and loads of other fun stuff.

So there I was, happily trotting along beside Richard and sniffing the air as we walked towards the beach, when I thought: "'ang on a minute, this air smells familiar. I've been here before, haven't I?". I couldn't quite place the exotic aroma of salty sea spray, joss-sticks, whiffy rubber wet-suits, and hundreds of 'messages' from Yorkshire Terriers that was blowin in the breeze. Then I got it. The breeze - that's it! It had to be El Blowo. "Great, now I'll be able to catch up with all my furry amigos in the town".

However, before I had the chance to reacquaint myself with all those exotic whiffs, I caught sight of a little white fluff-ball in the distance. I thought: "I recognise that fur and those cute little paws. Surely it can't be ... but yes it was ... Katy!"

Paws please, for the following romantic interlude ...

<CUE MUSIC, SOFT FOCUS, SLOW-MO ...>

She ran towards me across the empty beach, with the wind sweeping through her fur. I could hear her ecstatic woofing above the sound of the waves breaking, and the film score playing in my head. Richard released me from my lead, and we raced towards each other in slow motion and soft focus. My paws barely touched the ground - it felt like I was flying. The music built to an ear-shattering climax, the waves crashed onto the sand, and the camera zoomed in as we embraced.

<END ROMANTIC INTERLUDE>

So, was this just a clichéd dream sequence from some cheapo romantic novel? Of course not, I was nobody's Poodle, and nobody was going to spoil our reunion with a few cheap effects. We sniffed butt and licked each others noses like there was no tomorrow. I must admit my eyes were watering, but it must have been the feckin sand and wind.

Katy told me what had happened after she'd been picked up by the dog wardens: "they took me to the refuge and I was adopted by a lady who lives in El Blowo. Sally and her husband Kev have had lots of dogs before, but they were so sad when their last pooch died that they thought they couldn't bear to go through that again. That's until they saw me in the cage, and fell in love with me!".

I couldn't believe how things had worked out for the two of us. We'd both been through so much, and now here we were, together again on a beach in El Blowo.

She went on: "Sally and Kev are fur-tastic to me. I get fresh chicken and rice every day, I've got a lovely pink collar and lead, and loads of toys. They love me so much. I get cuddled all the time and groomed every day. You know how important that is for me. I need to look beautiful."

"I'm so happy for you Katy" I told her. "I was really upset and lonely when you disappeared into that van. I didn't know if I'd ever see you again."

"Same here" she sobbed. "Its wooftastic to see you again Gizmo. You helped me so much when I was on the streets. I probably wouldn't have survived without you."

Anyway, now we both lived in El Blowo we were sure to be seeing plenty of each other. All we had to do was to get our owners to be friends, and that would be easy when they saw what great amigos we were ourselves. So we said our hasta luegos to each other, happy to be living so close, and with such doggie-friendly humans.

Chapter Eight

I Woof therefore I Am

I settled in well with Nikki and Richard. As I thought, they didn't need much training to get the hang of the Gizmo routine, which basically just involves regular walkies, food, naps, and a spot of cat / ball / or squeaky chasing. Admittedly there were a few 'incidents' when I first moved in. Mostly involving chewing things that weren't designed to be chewed. After all, I was still a pup then (I'm in my prime now), and how's a pooch supposed to know which stuff you're allowed to chew, and which you aren't?

If you recall (or look back at chapter two), when I was living with Sharon and Trev I went through a phase of 'Compulsive Chewing Disorder'. I didn't really care what I chewed as long I could get it into my mouth and alter its shape in an interesting way, or even better, completely destroy it. It eventually led to my "Out-of-Botty Experience" at the vet.

This time it wasn't nearly so bad. My new humans actually gave me stuff that I was allowed to chew. They bought these specially designed chew-friendly items in the pet shop, and left them lying around for me in the living room. The only problem was that some of the other stuff there was rather more interesting than the designated chewable items.

The most expensive of these chewing incidents involved Nikki's watch. She'd left it on the coffee table - right in the 'chewing zone', so what did she expect? But hey, I shouldn't really blame her. She just needed a bit more training. Along with the watch, there were the three left shoes (for some reason they taste better than right ones), a bra, some swimming trunks, a rucksack, full box of tissues, and several loo rolls (OK, at last count, about forty-five loo rolls). These days I'm not into chewing so much. Maybe the odd loo roll occasionally just for old times sake, but if I see a tasty magazine just lying there on the coffee table, I usually have enough willpower to resist, now that I'm older and wiser.

Not long after settling into my new home I made a fantastic discovery. My amiga Katy was living just a few doors down the street from me! Even better, Nikki quickly became good friends with her owner Sally, so just as I'd hoped, we saw plenty of each other. Pretty soon we were going round to their house for coffee, and Katy and I would sit on the sofa woofing about the adventures we'd had together.

We'd certainly survived some tough times. Those bleak weeks when we struggled to find enough food and water to keep us alive; and even worse for Katy, whole months when she couldn't get to a groomer for her all-important fur-cut. I kept telling her that she looked lovely even without the grooming thing - the mutt's nuts, the dog's danglies in fact ... but it didn't really work, she was still well miffed. This obsession with grooming is definitely a bitch thing, and quite honestly I find them a complete mystery sometimes.

Talking about "ma bitches", I should tell you about this hot little Spaniel: Mercedes. I met her at the agility class, which is a sort of doggie gym. Nikki decided it would be a good idea for me to socialise with some other dogs and get even more excercise. As if I wasn't getting enough already, what with all my normal running, jumping and digging, but wadever, I wasn't bothered really.

Agility class is surprisingly good fun actually, and certainly very sociable. She chats with her human friends, and I get to hang out with my doggie mates and impress the lady woofers with my athletic prowess. We all take turns at jumping over the poles, balancing on the see-saw, and running through tunnels, but the real laugh is watching Nikki try to keep up with me. She's not exactly an Olympic athlete, my owner. Tries her best, but running is not really her thing.

Nope, Nikki and Richard were more into this funny surfing-the-wind thing that the humans did here in El Blowo. You remember I told you about it when Katy and I first got to the village (back in chapter three). They wore these strange outfits called 'wet suits'. Skin-tight black rubber gear which smelt well weird. There were always a few of these hanging around the house, and the more I sniffed them, the more

I liked them. Judging from the exotic aroma, these wet suits were wet from more than just salt water, and also seemed to be handy when the surfers were 'caught short'. Woof-Tastically whiffy!

Anyway, I digress. Let's get back to the agility class and "ma bitches". So, along with all the exercise stuff there was, of course, plenty of opportunity to sniff new butts and none was more sniffable than Mercedes' (woof woof!). I'd seen her before at doggie events, but she'd always ignored me. I think she was playing hard to get, but when she arrived at the class we got straight to the sniffing noses (and other orifices) stage, so I reckoned that I might be in there with a chance.

She was always the first on the equipment. In fact the instructor used her to demonstrate how it should be done. She had such style, finesse, and wow what a wooftastic butt! Then I had a go. No problemo of course. As you all know, I'm well fit and agile. After us the other woofers all took their turn, some more successfully than others, and of course there had to be one hooligan who couldn't help but pee on the equipment. Always has to be one doesn't there?

Mercedes was a bit of a tease though, and just when I thought I'd tickled her fancy with the combination of my finely tuned physique and super-sophisto 'new dog' brain, I realized that I might be barking up the wrong tree. Those gorgeous Spaniel eyes were focussed on another pooch called Sami. He was a great hulk of a hunting dog, nearly twice my size. I knew that I couldn't really compete with Sami. He was one hell of a mucho macho muvver, and big in all the right places - no bits missing; whereas as you already know, I no longer had my crown jewels intact. This was all a bit of a shame really. Mercedes and I could have made some beautiful puppies together, but hey ho, some bitches go for the macho, big-in-the-nether-regions kind of thing. They like a bit of 'ruff', whereas I'm more of your caring, sensitive, laid-back kind of woofer. As I say: a 'new dog' kind of dude in fact.

Luckily the bitches started paying me more attention once I started to get famous, and now that I'm a woofing celeb I have no problems attracting the lady poochettes. Quite the opposite in fact, I have to fight them off!

Ha ha, sprung that one on you a bit suddenly didn't I? I bet you're thinking "now hang on a dog-gone minute dude, did I miss something there? Famous? Celeb? Just when exactly did we get from being nobody's Poodle to some sort of super hero?". Well if you can just keep yer fur on for a minute, I'll tell you how it happened (still happening in fact).

The first step on my meteoric rise to stardom came when I took over the role of spokes-mutt for Nikki's website: TenerifeDogs.blogspot.com. This wooftastic blog aims to encourage more people to adopt abandoned dogs, and helps them find their perfect pooch. It has pages of useful information in the form of FAQ's, articles, and links, along with some success stories and of course lots of pics of my marvellous self, as well as all the hot news about what I've been up to. So please visit and bookmark TenerifeDogs ... but be warned - once you take a look at the cute doggies there, you may well find one leaps off the screen and tugs at your heart-strings, and before you know it you might have a new friend sharing your home!

The previous spokes-mutt, my predecessor: the late great Basil, was a hard act to follow, but I've grown into the role, and I think I've proved that I'm up to the job now. It's quite a responsibility as I have to be a role model and on my best behaviour all the time. I mean, it wouldn't do for the spokes-mutt to be caught peeing all over someone's leg or doing some other dastardly doggie naughtiness. OK, admittedly some of that does go on occasionally, but hey I'm only canine and sometimes a dog's got to do what a dog's got to do. I'm nobody's Poodle after all.

Nikki is quite handy with a camera, and one of my first tasks was to be the poster pooch for Marta's educational program. This involved visiting local schools, telling the children about the plight of stray mutts in Tenerife, and teaching them how to look after their pets properly. The posters tell the story of how I was abandoned, spent time as a homeless stray on the mean streets, and ended up being looked after in the refuge, before I was adopted. They show me giving the kids some tips on how to be a responsible dog owner, so that perhaps there might be fewer abandoned dogs roaming the streets in the future. By the way, you can find the posters, and some of my tips on the website: www.NobodysPoodle.com.

Posing for Nikki's camera was easy for a naturally talented poser like me. I love it in fact, and as you'll find out soon, her pics of my 'loveable mutt' features are all over the place now. You remember I told you how Katy and I loved to pose on Sally's sofa just like we were on Breakfast TV? Well when she saw how cute we looked, she sent a picture to the local newspaper: *Island Connections*, and before you could say "wag a tail" they signed me up to write a regular column and give the pooch perspective on things. We called it: *"Life According to Gizmo (It's a Dog's Life)"*.

It was a real honour to be the first dog to write for them (or any other newspaper?), and I do my best to be their intrepid News Hound, doggedly sniffing out the breaking news. Some of the treatment that gets meted out to my fellow dogs & bitches makes me barking mad and when I report it, I tell it like it is - no messing (or 'fouling' as the humans prefer to say). But it's not all shock-jock style reporting. I'm also a bit of a culture hound, and I try to keep my paw on the pulse of everything fun and funky in the canine world. If it's happenin' dude, then I'm tracking it, and as you know, us dogs are famous for our tracking skills.

We've always had our own methods for tracking things down. You humans use your clunky old computers when you want to search for something. You think you invented stuff like the Worldwide Web, Google, e-mails, social networking ... but what you don't realize is that us woofers have had this sort of stuff for ages. Not many people know this, but in fact we invented the idea of sharing information via a network (we called it the 'SmellNet'), along with on-line messaging ('SmellMail'), social networking ('SmellBook'), and wi-fi ('Wiffy').

When I leave the house for my walkies, the first thing I do is log-on (or 'sniff-on' as we call it) at the nearest lamp-post. There are other places to go online of course: trees, curbs, walls. They are the doggie equivalent of an internet cafe: public wiffy spots where you can sniff-on, check out your mates in smell-space (our equivalent of cyberspace), and just hang out, chill, and look cool.

Then I pick up my smell-mails, see what's been happening on SmellBook, and catch up with all the latest news and gossip. Who's dating who; how is Hugo the Yorkshire Terrier* getting on with his new prescription diet; and is Luna the Bulldog** still arguing with Speedy G ** the Jack Russell, over ownership of a bone they buried three months ago.

---

* remember him from chapter three? the 'babe magnet' Yorkie dude who was already slightly past his sell-by date? well lately he's been suffering from kidney stones that have unfortunately rather stymied his adventures with the babes.

** my cage mates from chapter five have been locked in a protracted disagreement that's been dragging on ever since they left the refuge, and will probably end up in court. Bone ownership rights are always tricky to settle in Canine law.

So, now I've sniffed-on and checked out what's been happening in local smell-space, I might add a comment or perhaps a 'like' by leaving a bit of pee on the lamp-post. Then I usually mosey on down to the wall near the rubbish bins. The wiffy signal is especially good there, and it gets a lot of 'hits', so it's always a good place to sniff-on and reach a big audience.

Anyway, that's how us dogs have been keeping in touch since the dawn of history, and it's only taken you humans a few millennia to catch up. You reckon you invented language, you like to to talk about the 'word of mouth', and for the past few decades you've had your internet to spread the word, but us dogs have been woofing and using the 'power of smell' to deliver messages since ... well, as I said, the dawn of canine history.

Of course in my role as a spokes-mutt for stray dogs I do often use the human internet, and especially FaceBook. My own page: Snr Gizmo has several thousand followers. There are loads of Nikki's pics of me there, and I'm getting some very flattering comments. Having a high profile online does have it's downside though. Along with all the SmellMail messages from my muttly fans, and the genuine mail that people send to Gizmo@TenerifeDogs.com, I also get my fair share of time-wasting e-mails. Now I'm as partial as the next mutt to a nice juicy can of spam, but these buggers are more like a can of worms.

For example, I got one recently from an African chap called Nadu Totow Savimbi. It's a very sad tale of how despite inheriting a lot of money, he's been unable to access his bank account, due to the overthrow of the government in his country. Nadu explains that he has twenty wives, seventy-eight children, and ten grandmothers to support, and that he desperately needs my bank account details, passport etc so that he'll then be able to transfer his late father's thirty-seven million dollar estate into my account. Of course he'll also bung me a few million quid just for letting him use my account and helping him with his extended family.

Woof-bloody-tastic, no? Sorry, but does Nadu really think I was born yesterday? and doesn't he understand that I'm a dog and unlikely to need a bank account? Honestly, I've said it before and I'll say it again - some humans must have fur for brains! I mean, why don't I ever get an e-mail from someone who says they're going to transfer two tons of dog biscuits to my bowl, just so that their dog can access it, as his own has been frozen. Now that would be talking my language, but realistically I suppose it's unlikely to happen. A dog can dream though, and talking of dreams ...

All this has got me thinking. My face is on posters, I'm writing a column for the local newspaper, and I'm all over the internet (both doggie and human). If I wrote my life story, surely it would bound to be a wooftastic success? I know I'm still a bit young to be a celeb, but then so were

Michael Jackson, Naomi Campbell, Wayne Rooney, and David Beckham (he's already 'written' three so far) when they had their autobiographies published, and how many have they sold? Ha, they needed ghost-writers to get in print (apparently Naomi admits she's never even read hers!). My humans certainly aren't ghosts. I mean, I could become a doggie legend just like Lassie, Marley, Scooby Doo ...

<START DREAM SEQUENCE ...>

I can just see it now: book signings, photo-shoots for the cover of 'Hello Bark' magazine, TV appearances, perhaps my own breakfast show co-presented with my furry amiga: 'Good Morning, on the sofa with Gizmo and Katy'.

Of course it wouldn't all happen at once. The book would start off as a bit of an underground cult thing, and the first signing party would be quite low-key. Just a few people and dogs in-the-know, somewhere intimate but quintessentially stylish. A few glasses of bubbly liquid, a few nibbles, a few of my muttly mates - actually they'll nibble anything and everything. You get the idea ...

(ps by the time you get to read this, you never know, there might actually be a YouTube video of my first book signing party, and if you look on the website: www.NobodysPoodle.com you might just find it there (but as we dogs say: "don't hold your breath") ... and by the way, could this possibly be the first ever novel by a promising new writer that actually comes with a description and video of the author's first book signing? How cool is that?)

In next-to-no-time (that's a dog's kind of time lapse) it would go from underground cult to mainstream hit, and the movie deal would be sure to follow. Before you can say "Hog-Warts-and-All" I'd be jetting off to Hollywood, trailed by paparazzi trying to hack into my phone (I bet they can't hack my iBone). And there's the rub, the downside of fame: no privacy to call your own. I'd have to start wearing dark glasses when I'm out and about. Beautiful bitches will be following me around offering to have my puppies (tough eh), and fans will want to camp outside my house and howl my name all night. Actually that might annoy Nikki and Richard a bit, best keep my address private.

Don't worry though, I'd keep my paws on the ground. I wouldn't let fame go to my head and give in to some of the stuff you read about celebs. No late-night biscuit scoffing, sniffing weird shit, mass humping sessions ... or at least, not *too* many anyway. Nope, I'd still be the same old Gizmo, just a bit more high profile - strutting my stuff on the red carpet, hanging out with ma bitches, posing for the paparazzi ... you get my drift ...

<END DREAM SEQUENCE>

Ah yes, a dog can dream, but before I get too carried away, I'd better finish this book (nearly there, as you can see). Now, what am I going to call it?

Well, my first thoughts were that I could go for the tabloid market, with a title that hints at lots of sexual shenanigans, maybe something like: '*Life's a Bitch!*'. I might sell a few on the back of that, especially with some saucy pictures, although I'm not sure that the illustrator would approve (eh

Annie?), and it's not really got much to do with my story has it?

Obviously I can't do Chick Lit, but perhaps I should go for the ex-pat diary / travel angle. It's always been a successful genre and inspired some mega best-sellers. Let's think now ... how about: '*Bouncing over Bones*' or '*More Saliva than Salsa*'?

Yep, now we're getting closer, but as you all know by now I've always fancied myself as a bit of an intellectual, or dare I say it myself, a canine philosopher. I'm forever stopping in the middle of a good sniff to ask myself deep and meaningful questions like: "if a dog barks his head off in the forest and no human hears him, is he still a bad dog?"; or "if I bury a bone so well that nobody finds it ever again, does it still exist?". So I was tempted to call my book something clever like: '*I Woof, therefore I Am*'. Deeply wooftastic eh? I mean, with a title like that they'd be bound to take me seriously, no? I'd be all over Radio 4 and Newsnight Book Review.

But then I thought: "yes dude, it's clever, but it's not very snappy, and maybe I can come up with something that *really* says who I am". OK for sure I'm a woofer so I woof, and therefore I am; and clearly I am, so therefore, obviously I woof ... and as you all know by now, I'm definitely an highly intelligent super-sophisto dog ... but who *is* this Gizmo? What's he *really* all about?

When it comes down to it, I'm more street Doodle dude than poncy Poodle, and I've always been my own dog. Never a stand-in for another dog. I'm all about standing up for the Underdog, even if it has got me into a few scrapes.

Aha, I'VE GOT IT ... as I've said all along:

I am Nobody's Poodle
But I'm Somebody's Doodle,
And I Woof ... therefore I Am!

About The Authors

NIKKI ATTREE studied photography at the University of London, graduating with a BA in 1987, before going on to work as a freelance photographer and digital artist in the UK. You can view her work on her website: www.NikkiAttree.com. Since moving to Tenerife in 2007, she has been helping to promote the hardworking animal rescue centres there by producing calendars and educational poster campaigns. Her website: TenerifeDogs.com is dedicated to finding homes for the island's abandoned dogs, as well as being a mine of information and an insight into the canine world. Despite being disadvantaged at school by mild dylexia and a woefully un-supportive English teacher, she has recently discovered an unexpected passion for writing. After years of feeling like a mobile Christmas tree or a heavily laden donkey, with state-of-the-art cameras and flash guns dangling from her every limb, it is refreshing for Nikki to do something creative without needing to be weighed down by tons of the very latest technology.

RICHARD ATTREE grew up in London in the 60's and left home as soon as he could to study a variety of useless subjects (philosophy), and play keyboards in various unsuccessful bands. For the next 25 years he made his living (sometimes sporadically) as a composer of music for TV, working at the BBC's renowned Radiophonic Workshop before going freelance with his own studio near Brighton. To hear some of his music visit his website: www.AttreeMusic.com. Tiring of the stresses of freelance life he decided to retire, sell up, and "downshift" to a sunny, windy beach on The Reef (Tenerife). Despite working for most of his life as a musician, Richard has always hankered after the straightforward, direct communication of language when struggling with the complexities of producing electronic music or hauling tons of keyboards up several flights of stairs. Retiring from the music business has given him the opportunity to get to grips with writing, as well as indulge in his other lifelong passion: windsurfing, which he and Nikki discovered together in the mid 80's and which has intervened heavily in their lives since. To read about their windsurfing adventures, and life on the Reef, check out their blog: LifeOnTheReef.blogspot.

GIZMO was abandoned on the mean streets of Tenerife when he was one year old, and spent some time in the Accion-del-Sol refuge, before being adopted by Nikki and Richard. The first step on his meteoric rise to stardom came when he took over the role of spokes-mutt for Nikki's website: TenerifeDogs.com. One of his first tasks was to be the poster pooch for Accion-del-Sol's educational program. This involved visiting local schools, telling the children about the plight of stray mutts in Tenerife, and teaching them how to look after their pets properly. Before you could say "wag a tail" he'd been signed up by Island Connections newspaper to be their intrepid news hound, doggedly sniffing out the breaking news and giving the pooch perspective in his regular column: 'Life According to Gizmo (It's a Dog's Life)'. After graduating with a diploma from the Star Agility class, he decided to share his story with a wider public by enlisting Nikki and Richard to ghost-write his first book: 'Nobody's Poodle'. You can find his posters, read his articles, and catch up with all the news about the book on www.NobodysPoodle.com as well as follow him on his Facebook page: Snr Gizmo. Besides his many other accomplishments Gizmo is an expert in woofing, sniffing, digging, chasing cats, siestas, and looking cute.

About The Illustrator

ANNIE CHAPMAN trained in Graphic design and illustration as well as Art and drama. She is originally from Lincolnshire in England but has spent over 20 years living and working in Tenerife and has worked as the principal Art teacher at a private British school in Tenerife for the past ten years, where she teaches art up to A-level. She has exhibited her artwork on the island and has illustrated two published books. Although primarily a cat-person Annie has thoroughly enjoyed getting to know Gizmo and his friends and is 100% pooch-friendly.

Printed in Great Britain
by Amazon.co.uk, Ltd.,
Marston Gate.